MW01639869

Virginia Avenel Henderson

Signature for Nursing

Mosby is proud to have had the opportunity to be a part of Sigma Theta Tau International's 75th Anniversary Celebration by donating the publishing services for this festschrift, and by contributing to the Virginia Henderson Clinical Research Endowment.

Virginia Henderson

Virginia Avenel Henderson

Signature for Nursing

Editor

Eleanor Krohn Herrmann, EdD, RN, FAAN

Professor
University of Connecticut
Storrs, Connecticut

Sigma Theta Tau International
Honor Society of Nursing

1998

Frontispiece photograph courtesy of Sherry L. Shamansky, DrPH, RN, FAAN.

Printed in the United States of America
Composition by Graphic World, Inc.
Printing/binding by Walsworth Publishing Co.

Sigma Theta Tau International
Center Nursing Press
550 West North Street
Indianapolis, Indiana 46202

Library of Congress Catalog Number 0-9656391-2-6

ISBN: 0-323-00249-8

For additional peer-reviewed titles published by Center Nursing Press, contact:
Sigma Theta Tau International
Honor Society of Nursing
550 West North Street
Indianapolis, IN 46202
1-888-634-7575
Fax (317) 634-8188

Views expressed herein are not necessarily those of Sigma Theta Tau International.

97 98 99 00 01 / 9 8 7 6 5 4 3 2 1

Contributors

Nettie Birnbach, EdD, RN, FAAN

Rev. William E. Bliss, MDiv

Billye J. Brown, EdD, RN, FAAN

Catherine M. Burdge, MSN, RN

Charles H. Burdge, Jr., MFA

Mary T. Foley Carew, MA, RN

Virginia Dericks, MA, RN

Nancy Dickenson-Hazard, MSN, RN, FAAN

Donna K. Diers, MSN, RN, FAAN

Mary Ellen Doona, EdD, RN

Melanie C. Dreher, PhD, RN, FAAN

Rhetaugh Graves Dumas, PhD, RN, FAAN

Meghan M. Fitzgerald, BA

Kathleen T. Flynn, MS, RN

Nelly Garzon Alarcon, MS, RN

Edward J. Halloran, PhD, RN, FAAN

Eleanor Krohn Herrmann, EdD, RN, FAAN

Daniel James, BS, RN

Lucie S. Kelly, PhD, RN, FAAN

Janet C. Ross Kerr, PhD, RN

Ruth N. Knollmueller, PhD, RN

Kazuko Kodama, BS, RN

Judith B. Krauss, MSN, RN, FAAN

Delia H. Mark, BA, BS, RN

Angela Barron McBride, PhD, RN, FAAN

Mildred L. Montag, EdD, RN, FAAN

Adele W. Pike, MSN, RN

Susan M. Reverby, PhD

Rhea C. Sanford, MSN, RN

Sherry L. Shamansky, DrPH, RN, FAAN

James P. Smith, OBE, MSc, SRN, RNT, FRCN, FRSH

Florence S. Wald, LLD, LittD, DMS (Hon); MN, MS, RN, FAAN

Morris A. Wessel, MD

Acknowledgments

Appreciation is expressed to Sigma Theta Tau International for conceiving this project and for its confidence in commissioning the editor. Gratitude is expressed to the individual contributors for their submissions and in some instances for recommending additional contributors.

E.K.H.

Foreword

N*ursing owes its development* as a profession to many of our predecessors; few, however, have been as influential as Virginia Henderson. Scholars have studied, researched, and written about nursing with significant contributions and results, but the definitive work of Miss Henderson's writings has been substantial in the development and expansion of current practice and education in nursing. I believe history will confirm her influence. It is appropriate that a collection of insights on Virginia Henderson and her influence on the profession will be published at about the time of what would have been her one-hundredth birthday. The writings are organized around three major themes: Virginia Henderson's leadership, scholarship, and humanitarianism.

The topics of the festschrift range from her influence on education to her qualities in mentoring. They are written from the perspective of family members, friends, colleagues, and students. Each is written from his or her personal knowledge of Virginia Henderson. The contributors write about her influence on nursing worldwide, specifically her influence on hospice nursing, research, mentoring, nurse executives, the practice of nursing, and the history of nursing. The offerings are amusing, sensitive to her as a person, and poignant, and they are purposeful, discerning, and resolute about a lady each of them knew somewhat differently. Yet each, in their presentation, brings out Miss Henderson's love of people, of nursing, and her determination to teach nurses to help the patient "maintain a healthy state of mind and body, or where a return of health is not possible, the relief of pain and discomfort."

Virginia Henderson was not a teacher in the classroom for me, but she was one of my teachers in my diploma nursing program. Miss Henderson and Miss Harmer were with me all the way, through their book, now a classic, *The Principles and Practice of Nursing*. Miss Henderson was there to answer my questions about every aspect of nursing, its practice and procedures. It was several years before I met Miss Henderson in person, and what a joy it was to finally meet this lady who had led me through many trials and tribulations in nursing school.

Later, when I was dean, I had the honor and privilege of having her visit our school of nursing as a distinguished lecturer. When invited, she told me that she did not "do speeches." This was fine, and one of my fond remembrances is of her sitting in a chair surrounded by students, faculty, and community persons in chairs or on the floor, wherever they could get as close to her as possible, to hear this very wise lady talk about nursing as she had known, lived, and defined it. Her definition has been the background for many nursing theories.

Another recollection I have of this diminutive lady was when she was in her nineties. I was visiting the Metropolitan Museum of Art in New York City and noticed a gathering of people standing in a circle. They were intently listening to someone who was standing in the center of the circle. My curiosity led me closer to the group and with some difficulty, by looking over many people, I saw it was Virginia Henderson. I waited for the session to end and asked her about her activities with these people. In her way, Miss Henderson explained that it was her birthday and one of her friends had brought her to the museum as a treat. She had been walking around seeing all that she could see when one of a group of people asked her a question about a particular exhibit. She said to me, "and I had to tell them about the exhibit and where they could go to see it!" Always a teacher! She had a keen sense of humor. She was a helping and caring person, which was demonstrated in many ways in her writing and in her daily activities. This random act of kindness was but one example of the human attributes of Virginia Henderson, a nursing legend and an international nursing treasure.

BILLYE J. BROWN, EDD, RN, FAAN
Dean (1972-89) and Professor Emeritus
University of Texas at Austin School of Nursing
Austin, TX
President (1989-91), Sigma Theta Tau

Editor's Preface

T*his festschrift is comprised* of descriptions of Virginia Avenel Henderson as perceived by different persons, each through the lens of their own mind's eye and life experience. Each description is a brush stroke. Together they suggest a portrait of one whose multifaceted richness of being defies complete depiction.

In every age a few great souls are sent to dwell among us. The radiance of Virginia Henderson's light allowed many to bask directly and indirectly in its rays, as she steadfastly went about her soul's business. She observed the near with profound insight; she measured the far with care and wisdom. Her path allowed others to follow where none had traveled before. Her vocation became the mirror of her soul. Her spirit, valiant to the end, helped an entire profession to find its own strength.

It is said that you cannot be your brother's keeper until you are your own. Virginia Henderson became her own keeper. She sought not applause or fame, but joyed in the recognition she was able to bring to her profession.

Virginia Henderson will be missed. Hopefully this collection will help bring her and her work to mind more often. As memories fade, the writings by and about Virginia Henderson will endure, a testament to a rare and noble nurse, whose boundless love, energy, and vision remain as a blessing to all humankind.

ELEANOR KROHN HERRMANN, EdD, RN, FAAN
Cheshire, CT
June 1997

Contents

Part III HUMANITARIANISM, *79*

Appendices, 107

Virginia Avenel Henderson

Signature for Nursing

Part I
LEADERSHIP

An Inspiration to Nursing Worldwide

Nelly Garzon Alarcon, MS, RN
Professor Emeritus
National University of Colombia Nursing School
Colombia, South America;
President (1985-89), International Council of Nurses

M***any nurses throughout the world,*** like myself, have been inspired by Virginia Henderson's definition of nursing. Her basic principles and concepts of nursing care, translated into more than twenty languages, changed the notion and practice of nursing. They also paved the way for theoretical statements formulated in the latter half of the twentieth century.

Those of us who learned nursing principles and practice from her text in the 1960s and who reflected on her writings about the nature and meaning of nursing developed admiration and fondness for her and a desire to know her personally. For many nurses, this was an impossible aspiration. For those of us who had the good fortune to do so, it was a marvelous and unforgettable experience.

Virginia Henderson and Florence Nightingale have been the two principal paradigms of inspiration in my professional life. These women marked fundamental moments in the history of nursing, and their writings continue to be a valuable source of wisdom.

As a member of the Board of Directors of the International Council of Nurses (1985-1989), I helped select the first recipient of the Christiane Reimann Prize, awarded at the 18th Quadrennial Congress of Nurses held in Israel in June 1985. This was a pleasant assignment, as the British Royal College of Nurses had wisely nominated Virginia Henderson. For me personally, and for the entire ICN Board of Directors, there was no doubt or difficulty in reaching a unanimous decision. Virginia Henderson had more than sufficient merit to warrant this distinction, and I believe she honored the ICN and the nursing profession by accepting the prize.

It was during the inauguration of the 18th Quadrennial Congress that many nurses from around the world had an opportunity to fulfill their dream of meeting Virginia Henderson. I was one of them. That evening, 88-year-old Virginia Henderson delighted an international audience of nurses with her youthful joy, her smile, her rose-colored dress, and her expression of fondness, friendship, and commitment to nursing. Radiating intelligence and great kindness, she stood like a small giant in the face of an enormous audience. Her words conveyed her tremendous charisma, dedication, and clear understanding of the essence of nursing.

Throughout the congress, nurses from around the world had an opportunity to speak with Virginia Henderson during formal meetings where she gave us guidance, exchanged ideas, and livened discussions with occasional comments reflecting her lively sense of humor.

Many of us came away with the intention of inviting her to our countries as a special guest. The Colombian members of the National Association tried to do so on several occasions but were unsuccessful. However, we were always in contact by letter, following her accomplishments, commemorating special dates, and reiterating our standing invitation for her to visit Colombia.

During my term as President of the ICN, I enjoyed reading accounts of her visit to Spain in 1988 where she brought together thousands of nurses who perceived her strength and her knowledge and listened to the clearness and foresight of her ideas on nursing progress. For young Spanish nurses, the vitality and enthusiasm of this 91-year-old nurse were contagious. They say nursing students looked on her with admiration and wanted to be near her, to touch her, as if she were a supernatural being with a message on the true meaning of nursing today. She moved them to think about the direction nursing should take in the future.

When I was President of the ICN, we maintained frequent contact with Virginia Henderson through our Executive Director, Connie Holleran, who called often, at least once a month, conveying our regards and affection. We sent flowers on her birthday and other special dates, which I know she enjoyed.

Our hope was that she would be here to celebrate her hundredth birthday, but such was not the case. Nevertheless, I am confident she lives on through her teaching, writing, and example as an exceptional woman and nurse.

In My Opinion

James P. Smith, OBE, MSc, SRN, RNT, FRCN, FRSH
Editor-in-Chief, Journal of Advanced Nursing;
Visiting Professor of Nursing Studies
Bournemouth University, Bournemouth, England

I ***was first made familiar with Virginia Henderson's views*** about nursing in the early 1960s as a newly qualified nurse tutor. The director of the school of nursing where I was employed gave me a copy of the ICN's *Basic Principles of Nursing Care.* It was only later that Virginia was formally identified as the author of the work (Henderson, 1968). Thereafter, that publication became my bible. I was so impressed with the simplicity—and profundity—of its message and the beauty of its jargon-free language. It excited me.

During a professional tour in Scandinavia in 1966, sponsored by the United Kingdom's National Florence Nightingale Memorial Committee, it was made quite clear to me that Virginia Henderson's influence was extended throughout Europe.

Virginia Henderson always refused to have her words about nursing endowed as a theory or concept. I am often amused by the attempts of some authors to identify Virginia Henderson with the body of nursing theorists. I know that that kind of academic activity would make her turn in her grave with anger. Virginia felt that the so-called nursing theorists would have made a more significant contribution to nursing if their theories had demonstrated some direct impact on the quality of nursing care delivered to real patients.

Over the years, I learned a great deal about Virginia Henderson from a mutual friend, Bethina A. Bennett, a British contemporary of Virginia's. Mrs. Bennett had recognized the importance of Virginia's contribution to nursing in the 1950s (Bennett, 1956). Virginia claimed that Mrs. Bennett showed an understanding of her work "that no other reviewer has ever demonstrated" (Henderson, 1980a).

It was Bethina Bennett who was instrumental in persuading Virginia to work for the ICN. Fortuitously, she became chairman of the ICN's Professional Services Committee. That marvellous ICN publication, now available in many languages, is a tribute to a great transatlantic friendship.

It was not until 1977 that I met Virginia for the first time. I was then the honorary treasurer for the Association of Integrated and Degree Course in Nursing (AIDCN), an organization that represented the university-level nursing programmes in the United Kingdom (UK). The AIDCN sponsored an annual Battersea Memorial Lecture, and the executive committee invited Virginia to give the 1977 lecture. As this was to be her first public appearance in the UK, we were all terribly excited, even though, as the AIDCN had no funds, it had to find resources to finance the visit.

In the end, everything worked out fine. On 4 November, 1977, Virginia Henderson gave an inspired presentation on "The Concept of Nursing." It was published later in the *Journal of Advanced Nursing* (Henderson, 1978). She spoke with lucidity, such conviction, and such humor, to a most appreciative capacity audience in the Nightingale School of Nursing, St. Thomas' Hospital, London. That was a most appropriate setting, for in a way, Henderson is the USA's Nightingale.

From that time on, Virginia and I established a firm and fruitful friendship. Her letters, always superbly written, were a pleasure to read. She seemed always to have had sight of my publications and, on occasions, honoured (and flattered) me by citing them. But, like all true friends, when she disagreed with me she was not slow to rebuke—in the gentlest possible way, of course.

After the 1977 lecture, Virginia took the rest of the UK by storm. She gave a series of seminars and presented papers in a number of parts of the country. She came back to the UK on a number of occasions after that, I am glad to say.

In 1978, she was created a Fellow of the Royal College of Nursing (FRCN) of the United Kingdom in recognition of her outstanding contributions to the art and science of nursing. That was a double pleasure for me, as I was created FRCN at the same time.

Virginia came to the UK again on 7 November, 1979 to give the Royal College of Nursing's annual lecture. She chose the theme "Preserving the Essence of Nursing in a Technological Age." She argued that "not until human beings are born, live and die in an independent state—and not until the special knowledge and skill of the nurse becomes common knowledge and skill, can we abandon what we think of as basic nursing care." That lecture, too, appeared in the *Journal of Advanced Nursing* (Henderson, 1980b).

We met up again in 1981 at the ICN Quadrennial Congress in Los Angeles, USA. She said she had come to "support" me as I was moderating the first plenary session at the congress. When I mentioned her presence to the several thousands of nurses attending the congress, they went wild with enthusiasm and applause.

Later she sent me a paper entitled "The Nursing Process—Is the Title Right?" (Henderson, 1982). In that paper she concluded that, because the nursing process stresses a dominant and independent function for the nurse, this may undermine the value of collaboration of health professionals and the development of the client's self-reliance. A subsequent publication by Walton (1986) suggested that some of the contentions in the paper were prophetic as far as the UK experience of using the nursing process was concerned.

Virginia Henderson was a great advocate of the patient's right to be involved in his/her own care. She often recalled that, in her own days as a teacher, she organized weekly "case reviews" with her nursing students, which the patients themselves attended and participated. She wrote a guest editorial once for the *Journal of Advanced Nursing*, demanding effective health records for everyone and pleading the case for all patients to have copies of their own health records. She was devoted to that cause (Henderson, 1986).

The most significant impact of Virginia's influence on me resulted from a commission from the Royal College of Nursing to prepare a short biography to mark her ninetieth birthday. I had the rare privilege of talking to her about her life whilst spending a few weeks at her home in New Haven. The interviews were recorded and subsequently the biography was published (Smith, 1989). It has already been translated into Finnish, Japanese, Italian, and Spanish.

She often expressed the view, which influenced me greatly, that nursing and nurses have been negatively affected by the influence of the social sciences in terms of orientation, research interest, and curricula development. There should be much more attention given to the biological sciences, she believed. I have the distinct impression that there is now a growing literature endorsing her concerns about the position of biological sciences in nursing curricula.

Virginia Henderson was a great advocate of health care funded from taxes; we both admired the British National Health Service. It saddened her that the USA, whilst supporting publicly-funded education, had never accepted publicly-funded health care. Those were also the views of her great mentor, Annie Goodrich, the first dean of the Yale University School of Nursing. Virginia regularly paid tribute to that remarkable public health nurse, pioneering army nurse, and outstanding educationalist. I shall always thank Virginia for introducing me to Miss Goodrich's writings (Goodrich, 1932/1973).

I was constantly amazed at Virginia's encyclopedic knowledge of professional, classical, scientific, and philosophical literature. She enjoyed well-informed, lively debate and discussion. Her dinner parties were often like enjoyable symposia. She always listened politely to others' views but readily offered her own "opinion." "Well, in my opinion . . ." she would say. Virginia often said that on her gravestone, the following words should be engraved:

IN MY OPINION
VIRGINIA HENDERSON
LIES HERE

Virginia Henderson was an outstanding nursing scholar, a remarkable nursing author, an esteemed international nurse, and a good friend to many. But, above all, in my opinion, Virginia Henderson was a charismatic, charitable, humble, happy, humane, and unique human being.

REFERENCES

Bennett, B.A. (1956). The unique function of the nurse. *Nursing Mirror, 103,* 939.

Goodrich, A.W. (1932/1973). *The social and ethical significance of nursing: A series of addresses.* New Haven: Yale University School of Nursing.

Henderson, V. (1968). *Basic principles of nursing care.* Geneva: ICN.

Henderson, V. (1978). The concept of nursing. *Journal of Advanced Nursing, 3,* 113-130.

Henderson, V. (1980a). Foreword. In J.P. Smith & P.A. Downie (Eds.), *A General Textbook of Nursing* (20th ed.). (pp. xv-xvii). London: Faber & Faber.

Henderson, V. (1980b). Preserving the essence of nursing in a technological age. *Journal of Advanced Nursing, 5,* 245-260.

Henderson, V. (1982). The nursing process—is the title right? *Journal of Advanced Nursing, 7,* 103-109.

Henderson, V. (1986). Some observations on health care by health services or health industries. *Journal of Advanced Nursing, 11,* 1-2.

Smith, J.P. (1989). *Virginia Henderson: The first ninety years.* London: Scutari Press.

Walton, I. (1986). *The nursing process in perspective: A literature review.* York: University of York.

Connections

Florence S. Wald, LLD, LittD, DMS (Hon); MN, MS, RN, FAAN
Branford, CT;
Dean (1957-68), Yale University School of Nursing
New Haven, CT

B***ecoming a colleague of Virginia Avenel Henderson*** in 1958 was by good fortune, a rare stroke of luck but not by design. There was a spacious office next to mine and space was what she needed. I was the young newly appointed Dean of the Yale University School of Nursing with little experience in academic nursing, little known in nursing circles, but sure and passionate that the school from which I graduated should survive and take its place in developing the art and science of nursing. Virginia and Leo Simmons had just finished a 5-year study and the writing of *Nursing Research: A Survey and Assessment,* which would be published in 1964. That review led her to the comprehensive unprecedented literature review, *The Nursing Studies Index: An Annotated Guide* of all reported studies, research methods, and historical and biographical materials in periodicals, books, and pamphlets published in English from 1900 through 1959. It would take until 1970 for all four volumes to be published. Meanwhile, as next-door neighbor for 10 years, I witnessed the industrious, cohesive interdisciplinary undaunted staff of librarians, secretaries, and nurse scholars pursue their collaborative interdisciplinary task in egalitarian team work. All were on equal footing with Virginia.

Their office was large, full of light, but institutionally sparse. Overnight it was transformed as drapes were hung, oriental rugs rolled out, original paintings hung, a working tea service and candy dishes placed to hide the gray metal desktops, and fresh flowers put atop the file cabinets. Despite the noisy corridor traffic, the door was usually open for all to see this humming model of scholars at work. Virginia often said she hated to write and had to think "glue" to keep her in the chair, but her writing was a delight to read, beautifully crafted, and clear. The annotation of each entry in the *Index* was concise and carefully cross indexed.

Those who never knew library search before computers, interlibrary loans, data bases, and surfing the web may find it hard to believe how carefully and widely she searched libraries near and far: trips to the New York Academy of Medicine, the libraries of Johns Hopkins, Columbia, Western Reserve, and the National Library of Medicine in Bethesda, Maryland.

By nature, Virginia loved books of all kinds; she also enjoyed people of all kinds. These two passions came together in introducing friends and colleagues to like-minded friends and colleagues in whom she perceived affinity.

Virginia entered nursing school the year after I was born, 1918. Annie W. Goodrich had been her mentor from her student days in the Army School of Nursing, also founded by Goodrich in World War I. Virginia said that Annie Goodrich believed Virginia saw nursing as an art. Yet Virginia was so meticulous and systematic in whatever she did, and was so knowledgeable in what systematic study encompassed, that she saw the scientist in her as well. Goodrich did not live to see the creation of the *Nursing Studies Index*, although she might have known before she died in 1954 that the survey and assessment of nursing research was underway. Both of us revered Annie Goodrich and Lillian Wald. She was fortunate to know them well; I was a distant admirer.

The strongest conceptual bond between Virginia and myself was first, that nursing knowledge comes out of nursing practice. The degree and way practice affects illness and the process by which wellness is achieved shape nursing principles. We both valued how the sociologist, Robert Leonard, taught master's-degree nursing students to delineate a clinical problem and test an approach to resolve it. Neither of us embraced nursing's search for theory or the complicated constructs and contrived vocabularies.

How fortunate I was to have that wise experienced colleague as my next door neighbor. Since she held a research appointment, she had no formal teaching or curriculum development responsibilities, but faculty, students, and I too, always felt we could go to her for advice.

Both faculty and student body were small from 1957 to 1968, but faculty had committed itself to redesign its curriculum on a trial basis. Closure of the basic nursing program now allowed faculty the freedom and time to start anew. Each member realized the risk being taken; no one had tenure and although few in number, there were traditionalists and innovators shaping curriculum. Having Virginia as critic and commentator in our microcosm as she was surveying the world-wide scene past and present, clarified and detonated tension. She was one of us but with the advantage of her up-to-the-minute worldwide review and appraisal of nursing literature, systematic study, and education elsewhere.

Meanwhile, our professional relationship flowed into friendship—the kind of friendship that was sound and stable enough to allow us to disagree and secure enough to think radically and shape new insights through discussion. When I married, she was one of our first guests. She instantly became best friend to my husband and his two children, then 6 and 8. Our first supper together was around our kitchen table in our new house even before other furniture was in place. Over the years she was with us for Passovers, Bar Mitzvahs, wedding receptions, and when grandchildren came to our house, Virginia was there too, bringing sweetmeats she made or an animal figurine from her flea market collection.

She loved our round dining room table where everyone could be included in conversation and nonverbal gestures. We could sit for hours. Her interests and concerns were so diverse, she was so well read, she expressed herself so clearly, and her sense of humor was so at the ready, discussing, for example, architecture, national health service, Gray

Panthers, Black Panthers, Buddhism, books, travel, Japan, Pakistan, Spain, France, England, Canada, movies, plays, ethics, social justice, biographies, and the visual arts. Mahatma Ghandi, the Dalai Lama, Thomas Jefferson, Woody Allen, Edmund Pellegrino, Cicely Saunders, Patricia Benner, Eleanor Roosevelt, and E.B. White were some of her heroes and heroines.

Delightful and stimulating as she was as a guest, she was an astounding hostess. Each of the three apartments she lived in, the first in New York and the last two in New Haven, were elegantly furnished with antiques. In the last one, the largest, there were seven rooms on the third floor where she lived until her ninety-fifth year. She gave credit to the three flights of stairs for keeping her active. Here her luncheon or dinner guests could be as few as one or as many as twenty. She was the cook, florist, arranger of seating, and major domo all in one, and an overall impeccable hostess. Sometimes the guests already knew each other, a reunion of old friends; at other times she brought people together whom she thought had interests in common. What she did for the nursing profession in bringing nurses together by annotating their writings so that nursing professionals could find one another through a published index, she also did with friends, colleagues, and students in her leisure time, introducing like-minded people or people with shared interests to each other.

I was a most fortunate beneficiary of her talent. It was Virginia Henderson who introduced Cicely Saunders to me. Virginia had already read Saunder's "Care of the Dying," published in *Nursing Times* in 1957, so when she discovered Dr. Saunders would speak at Yale's Medical School in 1963, she saw to it that I heard her. The impact of that meeting was tremendous. Virginia knew how troubled and helpless I had been seeing patients with cancer inexorably treated with surgery and radiation beyond the point of remission, while pain and suffering escalated—and without their questions and their family's questions being answered. It was this meeting that planted the first seeds of the hospice movement in United States soil and allowed the first interdisciplinary team to be developed. Here it was initiated by nursing. Virginia in the 1990s would call the concept "the epitome of nursing." She ultimately played a significant role in its development. She served on two committees in the planning stage: one proposed elements of patient-family care; the other searched for an architect, and ultimately a site.

From 1971 through 1975, Virginia worked with the architect, Lo-Yi Chan, an experience she relished. Lo-Yi and Virginia enjoyed and respected one another. Virginia's love and skill in creating settings and decorations came to the fore.

Meanwhile, Virginia and I were engaged in revising Chapter 50, "Death and Dying" for the sixth edition of Henderson and Nite's *Principles and Practice of Nursing.* In the 23-year span from the fifth to the sixth edition, care of the dying had advanced from a handful of references to a rich interdisciplinary bibliography that emanated from Herman Feifel's *The Meaning of Death* in 1959, Cicely Saunder's founding of St. Christopher's Hospice in 1967, and Elisabeth Kübler-Ross's 1969 publication, *On Death and Dying.* In that time, the hospice movement that had begun in England was being transplanted from there to Canada in the form of palliative care units and to hospice care in the United States.

Despite the host of new facts, findings, and thought generated in that span of time, Virginia's earlier 1955 version of "Death and Dying" already held many of the same elements that were yet to come: death as a normal part of life, the views of novelists (such as

Leo Tolstoy) and philosophers (Michael Montaigne), and the multifaceted nature of spiritual support. In the earlier edition she had already cited the teachings and writings of William Osler and Alfred Worcester on the physician's role with dying patients. The sixth edition did not refute the fifth edition but used it as a foundation, as if it were purposely built for what was to come.

In the final three years of her life, Virginia's vibrant life took a sudden turn from being always ready and able to travel in the United States and abroad; from active correspondent, lecturer, and writer; from caring for family members and friends in illness; from being the life of every party; from delighting in taking untrodden paths; overnight, all that changed beginning on a return trip from France in 1993. She didn't ask for help but when asked if she wanted help, she said she needed it. She accepted it without embarrassment. It was now a time for others to provide it as best they could. She appreciated helping hands and rarely railed at her dependence. She did have to move.

There was a rental apartment in a suburb of New Haven, with dining and assisted living services. Her family brought her carefully chosen belongings that transformed the one-bedroom space into a miniature of her last seven-room one. She had approved the place before it was leased. She said it was remarkable, and she relished having all her "stuff" around her. She was frank but not complaining of her "incarceration." She felt safe, and that was worth the price.

I marveled at her acceptance of this change. Not being able to converse, read, or hear well was so foreign to her life-style. There were bursts of frustration and anger, but these were short-lived. She loved the aide's affection and respect for her, the visitors (especially the children), the chocolates, the flowers, and the gin and tonic. She had a few falls, some aches and pains, but she said "I feel normal." The only sibling of eight still alive, her sister Frances Houff came from Lexington, Virginia twice each year. "Precious visits," Virginia had often said. "Frances knows me better than anyone."

A last public appearance was at the Connecticut Nurses Association Annual Meeting in 1994. When she came into the room, the audience rose to their feet and clapped endlessly until she took her seat at the head table. For a few hours, amazingly she was her old self.

Once she became too frail to walk about, she went to the Connecticut Hospice, whose services and space she had helped design. It wasn't her home; her appetite dwindled, but she still relished Godiva chocolates and ice cream. A medical exam found her to be well and dying in good health. She rarely needed medication.

Over her hospice bed there was a photograph of four little Hendersons: Jane, Virginia, Frances, and Lucy taken at the turn of the century. Virginia was full of bounce—as she had been through most of her life. She had followed her own path with wisdom and the courage to take risks. She relished the twelve honorary degrees awarded her. She knew as everyone around her did that she certainly earned them. It was not only that academia honored her, but it honored nursing. She loved to see younger colleagues receive their honors due.

We sometimes talked about one regret. She had not married. What a supportive wife, a loving, capable mother, an animated hostess, a wise grandmother she would have made. Even in her eighties and nineties, men and children were drawn to her. A terrible loss to one man, one family, and her personal fulfillment. But what an inspiration, what a model and joy to humanity.

On Mentoring

Rhetaugh Graves Dumas, PhD, RN, FAAN
Vice Provost Emeritus for Health Affairs;
Dean Emeritus, School of Nursing;
Lucille Cole Professor of Nursing
University of Michigan
Ann Arbor, MI

T***o speak about my relationship with Virginia Henderson***, I am impelled to convey the broadest possible meaning for the term *mentor.* For me, Virginia was much more than the wise, experienced, trusted advisor, and advocate generally ascribed to this term.

We met in 1959 at a welcoming reception for new students at Yale University School of Nursing. I was delighted to meet the author of *Principles and Practice of Nursing,* the major textbook for my basic clinical courses when I was a student nurse and an essential reference source following graduation. I was overwhelmed by my anxiety, given the magnitude of changes in my life attendant to this new venture, and by the awe inspired by Virginia's presence. But talking to her for only a short while put me at ease. I am sure that it was what she conveyed by her manner—because I don't remember a word that she said—that made me feel that she was someone who would be interested in my welfare as a new student, a black person in a predominately white institution, far removed from my upbringing in the deep South, and a single parent of a daughter only five years old.

Although very difficult to describe in precise detail, the relationship that evolved between Virginia Henderson and me could well be viewed as an exemplary model, a moral paradigm if you will, for advancing the nature and quality of human relations in all walks of life—especially in those communities where we expect to expand levels of mutuality and foster learning and growth and leadership. There were no prohibitions on what we could talk about, nor were there restrictions on the kind of social engagements we might share. So her influence pervaded both my personal life and my career development. Indeed her involvement at critical junctures in my life enabled me to advance progressively in my work even in the face of difficult challenges. Two poignant examples come to mind.

Knowing how deeply I would be touched by the assassination of President Kennedy, Virginia wanted to be the one to break this tragic news to me. Unable to find me in the School of Nursing, she came to the restaurant a block away where I was having lunch. I don't remember what she said, but I do remember that it was enormously helpful to have her there as I struggled to recover from the initial shock. Similarly, when Martin Luther King was assassinated, Virginia was there acknowledging my pain, my sorrow, and my rage. She revealed her own feelings and shared with me her philosophical anchors for such turbulent times. This she did not only in person, but also in a long letter that I could read when ever I was inclined to give up hope for the goals for which Dr. King's life was sacrificed. In times such as those, Virginia's attention and counsel provided me the inspiration and motivation to move beyond the anger and despair that I experienced and to view my own goals and ambitions for my life's work within a more favorable perspective.

I appreciated enormously Virginia's indulgence in matters that others were likely to see as extravagant or frivolous. Her own elegance in her work and in her social life gave credence to my efforts to balance work and play, such that neither the diligence demanded by my academic responsibilities, my attention to aesthetics, nor my time for lively and exciting entertainment, would be precluded one by the other. I learned from Virginia how to enjoy elegance without guilt. The receptions and special parties that she planned were carried off in grand style, complete with background music by a string ensemble, ice sculptures, delectable food (some prepared by herself), a wonderfully diverse mix of interesting people, and one of the world's most gracious hostesses.

I could trust Virginia to be frank and direct in our communications. She was one of my most severe critics, never hesitant to tell me when she thought that I was wrong on certain issues, that my arguments or conclusions in some situations were not valid, or that a piece of work representing hours of diligent effort was not good enough.

She was also liberal in the assistance that she provided, in the potent encouragements for the goals and ambitions that I sought, and in her expressions of admiration and praise when they were due. She was not reluctant to share her musings, her frustrations, revelations from her personal story—including new insights as well as the wisdom gleaned over her life's journey. And so our relationship reflected a level of mutuality that was unfettered by issues of status or power or individual prerogatives. It was a relationship of mutual respect, of caring, and of sharing, which deepened progressively our love for one another.

Having Virginia Henderson as a mentor of this order greatly enhanced my capabilities as a nurse and scholar, strengthened my capability as a writer, advanced the nature of my contributions in health care and health policy arenas, enabled me to develop my person as one that I have continued to appreciate and enjoy and, above all, established in my fondest memories her indelible legacy for a long life of enrichment and ennoblement as a member of the nursing profession and a woman of the world.

A Japanese Perspective

Kazuko Kodama, BS, RN
Professor
Japanese Red Cross College of Nursing
Tokyo, Japan

I***t started with her book*** *Basic Principles of Nursing Care.* It was my wedding day, May 1, 1961. We were at the wedding dinner table when Miss Masu Yumaki, my teacher and mentor, arrived direct from the airport. She had just returned from Melbourne, Australia, where she attended the ICN Congress as representative of the Japanese Nursing Association (JNA). She was then the JNA president. She looked very much excited and handed me a copy of a postcard-size booklet, saying that I should start a Japanese translation of the book right at once. The title of the book read *Basic Principles of Nursing Care.* It always amuses me to recall that it was several days later that Miss Yumaki gave me a piece of opal as my wedding gift. She said she forgot to hand it to me at the wedding party.

Miss Masu Yumaki was then the head of the nursing faculty of the Division of Health Care and Nursing, which was opened in 1953 in the School of Medicine, Tokyo University. I was a graduate of the class of 1955 and soon joined the faculty, also serving as Miss Yumaki's research assistant.

Miss Yumaki and I often discussed the study of nursing—whether nursing could be a subject of academic pursuit, and if so, what would be its body of knowledge. She made it a rule to talk to me perhaps because I was the youngest of the nursing faculty then and I tried to make myself always available to her. She shared every piece of her knowledge and thought with me so that in the course of time I found myself capable of joining her murmuring to herself.

Miss Yumaki was in a great dilemma at that time. The general opinion of the faculties at the Tokyo University was that nursing was not a full-fledged discipline and did not deserve to be the subject of academic study in such a prestigious higher educational institution as Tokyo University. The students, on the other hand, were greatly disappointed with what they were studying, which they thought could hardly be called a science.

Nursing was taught us as fragments of care activities. We were not aware that the nursing care we practiced in the hospital was a part of nursing study and that what we were practicing would ultimately constitute nursing's body of knowledge. We thought that there should be somewhere a dignified study of nursing that was totally different from what we actually practiced in the hospital. Our misleading idea was further misdirected by some of the faculty members who told us that we were supposed to become nurse administrators and educators and not to become nurses who work in clinical settings.

I knew Miss Yumaki was frustrated. She knew the value of nursing but she did not know how to put it in words. In *Basic Principles of Nursing Care,* she found the exact words that she was searching for in order to convey her thoughts on nursing. She was excited to read the principles of nursing care as presented there, which made all the nursing activities meaningfully related to each other. The book revealed an image of the science of nursing before us. It dawned on us that the science of nursing had been there in front of us all the time but we just could not recognize it. She was so anxious to share this understanding with Japanese nurses.

The Japanese translation of *Basic Principles of Nursing Care* was published in October of the same year. I was also as excited as Miss Yumaki while translating the book. It would be no exaggeration to say that this excitement was contagious for all the nurses who read the Japanese translation. Once they realized the principles, they were able to provide nursing care with more confidence. They ceased to indulge in arguing, "What is nursing?" Then it followed that the domain of nursing science came to shape itself. I will not go into details of the changes we experienced then, because I believe this process of change must have been experienced by all nurses in the world who read *Basic Principles of Nursing Care.*

Five years after this, Miss Yumaki received a copy of *The Nature of Nursing* directly from Miss Henderson. We both read it eagerly, and the Japanese translation was soon published. Among so many books on nursing theories published in Japanese translation to this date, nothing can still compare with these two writings of Miss Virginia Henderson in terms of the number of nurses who read these books and have been influenced by them.

I tried to read all the writings of Miss Henderson published in nursing periodicals in the United States and in the UK, and translated as many as I could. The more I read Miss Henderson, the more I was impressed and devoted to her. I was struck by the wide dimensions of her thoughts on nursing, her clear-cut yet discreet definition of the uniqueness of nursing, her emphasis on discipline and manners in nursing, her sense of actuality, and her aesthetic sense.

In the autumn of 1981, I was traveling on the east coast of the United States with my crew to make audiovisual teaching material on the history of American nursing. During this trip I had the chance to talk to some of the American nurses about my respect for Miss Henderson. Encouraged by their advice, I took it upon myself to visit Miss Henderson at her house on Linden Street in New Haven.

Miss Henderson received us most warmly, and she treated us with cookies and sandwiches that she made for us. Quite unexpectedly, she kindly agreed to appear in our film interview. In the last part of the video film *Nursing in the United States,* she talked to the Japanese nursing students, saying that nursing is one piece of chain in the total health care chain, and that if that part is weak, the strength of the total health care chain will be limited.

Miss Virginia Henderson visited Japan in 1982 at the invitation of the Japanese Nursing Association celebrating its thirty-fifth anniversary. Thousands of nurses who filled the large conference halls in Tokyo and Kyoto where Miss Henderson's lectures were given were excited and charmed by her. Miss Henderson answered every question until her voice became hoarse. Those who were fortunate to ask questions of Miss Henderson expressed how much they were inspired and encouraged by her writings.

I was then the editor-in-chief of the Japanese Nursing Association Publishing Company, and I was privileged to accompany Miss Henderson throughout her stay in Japan. How precious was the time with her, looking out of the windows of the Bullet Train, walking through the temples in Kyoto or the campus of Tokyo University, in Kabuki Theater, in a department store or on a downtown shopping street, or sometimes in her room at the hotel! We enjoyed talking, or rather listening to her, about her family and her colleagues at Yale, about reading books, about needlework and cooking that she loved so much . . . and of course about a lot of more serious subjects.

I also translated some works of Florence Nightingale. In *Notes on Nursing,* Miss Nightingale says, ". . . what nursing has to do . . . is to put the patient in the best condition for nature to act upon him." It was my understanding that "the best condition" could be interpreted as satisfying fundamental human needs, maintaining physical and emotional balance, and promoting independence, as Miss Henderson described in her writing. It was my understanding then that after one century's progress of human wisdom, Miss Henderson was able to develop the concept of "the best condition" in this way. In other words, I thought Miss Henderson rediscovered Miss Nightingale. I told this to Miss Henderson.

Miss Henderson said she was interested to know my point of view. But what I realized from her then was that she discovered the principles of nursing from her own exploratory practice of nursing as a nurse, just as Miss Nightingale discovered her nursing from her own experience in Crimea. Then we both agreed that *Notes on Nursing* would not have provided us the exact answer to "what is nursing" in 1960 when Miss Henderson published her book, because of the tremendous progress in natural and social sciences since Miss Nightingale's time and because of the recent changes in the health care system, which operates on multidisciplinary team work.

I revisited New Haven with my friend in April, 1988 to attend the lecture and party to celebrate Miss Henderson's ninetieth birthday, hosted by Yale School of Nursing. We were offered the special privilege of visiting her home twice during our stay. Mr. James P. Smith was staying there as her guest to write her biography. We translated his book *Virginia Henderson: The First Ninety Years* into Japanese, and it is read by Japanese Hendersonians with great interest. I think this is an interesting work from the standpoint of development of the nursing science.

The party at Yale University was an exciting experience for me. I was strongly impressed when Sister Callista Roy told me that she learned many things from Miss Henderson. I made new acquaintances whose major interests were in the history of nursing, including Dr. Eleanor K. Herrmann, who kindly invited me to contribute to this festschrift.

"There is nothing physically wrong with Miss Henderson, so we will see each other at her hundredth birthday," someone said at the party. But it was different. When the birthday card I sent her was returned, I knew that she no longer lived at Linden Street. A number of my acquaintances kept me informed about how Miss Henderson was doing, and I was glad to know that she was able to continue her style of living. I was deeply moved that Miss Henderson was always under the loving care of her family, the faculty of Yale School of Nursing, and her friends. I talked to the editor of one of the Japanese nursing periodicals about publishing an issue devoted to Miss Virginia Henderson, and this was published in January, 1996.

I was hoping to meet Miss Henderson again during summer vacation but the sad news came earlier. To the best of my ability and with my whole heart, I contributed a "Bio-bibliography of Virginia Henderson" to the official journal of the Japanese Nursing Association.

On May 6, 1996, I visited New Haven for the third time. The Yale School of Nursing had moved to a new building but Dean Krauss and the faculty had a beautifully arranged room there to remember Miss Henderson forever. All the words spoken and music played at the memorial service at the Battell Chapel sounded to me like "Virginia Henderson forever." It still echoes in my ears.

Cultural Bridge to Modern Nursing

Donna K. Diers, MSN, RN, FAAN
Annie W. Goodrich Professor;
Dean (1972-85), Yale University School of Nursing
New Haven, CT

My ***favorite memory of Virginia*** is the year she received an honorary degree from Yale, an event she called her "coronation." In addition to the commencement ceremony at which honorary degrees are actually conferred, there is an elegant dinner the evening before, black tie. The dinner is preceded by a cocktail hour in the President's home, a beautiful Federalist building on the Yale campus. The party walks a half block up Hillhouse Avenue to a mansion used now as a classroom building, which has a dining room large enough to accommodate the crowd. There are fresh flowers, several wines, lightly humorous academic toasts, place cards, and cigars for the men.

Virginia was there in pink and green satin, looking even more like a pixie than usual. She set herself up in the curve of the Steinway concert grand piano in the President's living room and received tall, handsome, important men who took advantage of the piano to drape themselves smaller so they could speak directly to her. She was seated at dinner between Kingman Brewster, former president of the University and then Ambassador to the Court of St. James, and the then-dean of the art school, the painter Andrew Forge, an Englishman, and she charmed them throughout dinner. She was in her element.

That—the element—is what I always associate with Virginia. Graciousness, civility, a sense of privilege and entitlement, charm, a kind of southern female fearlessness inherited from generations of strong women who tamed strong men. It is a personal style I could not possibly mimic or even learn, but I watched her work her magic over and over and envied the ability.

Everything she did, she did *thoroughly.* There were never loose ends, even if she had to involve an army of volunteers to do what needed to be done. A dinner party was an orchestrated symphony, a "salon," a privilege for her guests. Her writing—she never learned to type (or to drive, for that matter)—even in rough draft was crafted to the precise point, clearly expressed, without embellishment. And nearly impossible to read in the flowery penmanship she grew up with.

And when one received a note commenting on something one had written that she liked, it was tucked away in the secret folder kept for personal goodnesses. Her note writing was legendary, nearly approximately Florence Nightingale's productivity, but much kinder than Miss Nightingale's often acerbic prose.

Virginia was, for me, the cultural bridge to the beginnings of modern nursing. She was born when Miss Nightingale was still alive, making all of us who knew her only one nursing generation from the founder. She brought Miss Nightingale alive in her own writing and sent many of us chasing down *Notes on Nursing* or some more obscure Nightingale citations Virginia knew intimately.

When I first met Virginia, in about 1962, she was finishing the monumental *Nursing Studies Index* project. She worked in a large sunny room in the Yale School of Nursing with her assistants, two other older ladies. There were always fresh flowers about, an oriental rug on the floor, real teacups, and a huge grey bin of IBM cards in the middle of the room. I did not appreciate the significance of this work until much later. Remember, the *Index* is an annotated collection of the nursing literature to 1960. When I think about how difficult this was for the time, without computers or MedLine searches, not even good mimeographing capacity, it is an astonishing commitment to nursing scholarship that influenced me greatly when *Image* began to review and publish "State of the Science" articles.

Truth to tell, Virginia and I did not like each other very much. We were civilized and occasionally even warmer than that, but I was a rough lump of coal compared to her Hope diamond. When I was one of the early faculty members at Yale to wear pants to work—it simply wasn't done—the expression on her face when she saw me did not need translation.

I respected Virginia enormously for many things, but especially for the definition of the unique function of the nurse and the translation she did of it, which is less well known:

> [The nurse] is temporarily the consciousness of the unconscious, the love of life for the suicidal, the leg of the amputee, the eyes of the newly blind, a means of locomotion for the infant, knowledge and confidence for the young mother, the [voice] for those too weak or withdrawn to speak. (Henderson, 1964, p. 63)

That description and the related ones Florence Nightingale wrote that emphasize the kind of anticipatory, behind-the-scenes, invisible, stage-management work of nursing have profoundly affected my professional practice not only in caring for patients, but in working to shape the systems of care and the data by which they might be changed.

It was very special to have known Virginia in so many forums that those who only read her writing or have heard her speak once or twice did not have. She was a complex woman, unafraid of showing her complexity. Her standards for everything and everybody were very high and she lived up to them all.

Reference

Henderson, V. (1964). The nature of nursing. *American Journal of Nursing, 64,* 62-68.

About Nurse Executives

Edward J. Halloran, PhD, RN, FAAN
Associate Professor
University of North Carolina School of Nursing
Chapel Hill, NC

The three nurse executive positions I held were interspersed with three educational opportunities. The first position was in a rural hospital in Connecticut and came after I completed an undergraduate degree program designed for nurse graduates of hospital schools. The second was at a hospital in a suburb of Chicago and followed my master's degree. After completing a doctorate in nursing, I was appointed nurse executive at a large, urban hospital in Ohio. In each of these positions, I found myself spending more and more time with other leaders in the institutions: physicians, administrators, and board members. There was also less time to spend with an increasing number of nurses. While Virginia Henderson provided me the tools necessary to communicate effectively with these disparate groups, it was not until the third position, and after in-depth study of nursing, that I realized the extent of her guidance.

The forces that pull on nurse executives today approximate the demands made on any health care system. They are the need to provide medical and nursing care and administer them in a way that maximizes effect and minimizes cost. While there is controversy about how to accomplish this task, it is even more complicated when adjuvant tasks like teaching and research are performed without immediate benefit to the patients being served. Each of the dominant players—doctors, nurses, and administrators—have distinct ideas about the best way to accomplish the primary goal, effective and efficient patient care. I depended on Miss Henderson's clarity of expression to help simplify what has become the nightmare of interlocking legal, economic, medical, and social issues in healthcare.

Her writing on the function of the nurse set the tone for my leadership in a practice profession. It reads:

> The unique function of the nurse is to assist people, sick or well, in the performance of those activities contributing to health, its recovery (or to a peaceful death), that they would perform unaided if they had the strength, will or knowledge. And to do this in such a way as to help them gain independence as rapidly as possible. (Henderson, 1960/1997, p. 4)

The prominence of patients and helping them gain independence were essential objectives for the nurses to achieve. While each nurse had a way to express what he or she was doing for patients, it was necessary to have a message that could be communicated among nurses, to patients, and to doctors and administrators. Henderson's language was the only one that could be spoken to, and understood by, each of the different audiences.

It was not sufficient to have a description of nursing. It was also necessary to address the objectives of administrators and physicians. Administrators were most interested in the efficiency of operations, and physicians were dedicated to diagnosing and treating disease among the patients served. These objectives were sometimes seen as being at odds with the aims of nurses.

Efficiency has been the primary responsibility of managers. They have employed principles of scientific management since Taylor published them at the turn of the twentieth century. An objective of management is to gain efficiency by substituting more expensive procedures with less expensive ones of equal quality. This has been achieved in hospitals by replacing workers with technology and by dividing work into tasks that can be allocated to workers of differing skill and cost. The work of nurses has been studied for much of this century for ways it could be allocated to staff members less costly than nurses. Most staffing methodologies employ techniques that describe nurses' work in procedural terms and classify patients as capable of being cared for by aides, practical nurses, or professional nurses—that is, caregivers who could safely perform tasks for one or another patient group.

Henderson saw the procedure in quite another way. She argued it was knowledge and skill to be transferred from the nurse to the patient. In her view the task was not an end in itself but a means to patient independence. Safe performance of a procedure was not enough; some means had to be employed to enable patients to resume responsibility for their own care. Henderson promoted the use of two methods: support and encouragement, and patient education. It is only becoming known that care can be much more efficient when more of the responsibility for it rests with the patient and family. Brooten and Naylor (1995), Nite and Willis (1964), and others have tested Henderson's description of nursing and have found care to be less costly and more effective than that given "efficiently" in institutions. I found many administrators surprised to discover that methods of scientific management resulted in more costly care than that provided by professional nurses.

The language of physicians dominates hospitals today. Even nurses describe themselves as orthopedic or cardiology nurses, not as nurses who work in these hospital locations. Diagnoses and treatment seem paramount in all health care functioning. The first question about any patient today is, "What disease does he suffer from?" (Even more perverse is, "What diagnosis related group [DRG] is the patient in?") It is presumed that all subsequent patient information will emanate from the diagnosis.

Miss Henderson saw diagnoses in quite another way. In fact, they were not mentioned in her *Principles and Practice of Nursing* text (1978/1997). Diseases, per se, were considered less important than was the impact of the diseases on patients. Diseases were not as significant as the pathological states that sometimes accompanied them. Symptom management was essential for good patient care and was a function of the nurses who were with the patient at all hours. Diagnosing and treating were also essential for effective hospital work but were the primary responsibility of physicians. The distinction was necessary if the work doctors and nurses did for the same patients at the same time was to be complementary. Even when work once performed by physicians was to be considered for nurses, I used the criteria that distinguished therapeutic from diagnostic work and incorporated the former into nursing practice. The diagnostic work was to be accomplished by technical staff at the direction of physicians. I found doctors surprised by the use of a textbook to adjudicate disputes about overlapping functions. They were comfortable with the process but surprised at the size and scope of the textbook.

Drucker (1988) depicted the hospital as a prototype of the twenty-first century's successful organization. He said that the hospital, like the symphony orchestra, consisted of a group of knowledge workers who all had specialized functions. They did not speak much with each other, but they were all dependent on one another to produce the coordinated service that patient care has become. Virginia Henderson provided me the wherewithal to fully participate as a nurse in hospital management. Her contributions are still available, and their use makes the complex job of speaking to so many audiences at once less daunting. I was half way into my professional life as a nurse executive before I discovered the value of her writings. Perhaps others can benefit from them earlier in their careers.

References

Brooten, D., & Naylor, M. (1995). Nurses' effect on changing patient outcomes. *Image: Journal of Nursing Scholarship, 27*(2), 95-99.

Drucker, P. (1988). The coming of the new organization. *Harvard Business Review, 66*(1), 45-53.

Henderson, V. (1960/1997). *Basic principles of nursing care* (Rev. ed.). Geneva: International Council of Nurses.

Henderson, V., & Nite, G. (1978/1997). *Principles and practice of nursing* (6th ed.). Geneva: International Council of Nurses.

Nite, G., & Willis, F. (1964). *The coronary patient: Hospital care and rehabilitation.*New York: Macmillan.

Speaking Words of Wisdom

Sherry L. Shamansky, DrPH, RN, FAAN
Formerly Vice President for Nursing
Group Health Cooperative of Puget Sound
Seattle, WA

I ***first met Miss Virginia Henderson*** in 1967 while I was a graduate student at the Yale School of Nursing. When I returned to Yale in 1981 as a faculty member, we renewed our acquaintance, which then evolved into a friendship. Over the years I had the rare privilege to know this woman who touched my life and career in a profound way. The events that are described in this vignette span almost a decade, yet the themes are quite consistent: her enormous intellect; her sense of social justice; her ability to engage others with her wit, grace, and humor; her unabashed caring for people's fundamental needs; her ability to speak the truth and simultaneously "push the envelope," and more. Whenever I have found myself in a predicament at work, I step back and ask myself, "What would Virginia do now?"

In 1985, Virginia Henderson was the recipient of the first Christiane Reimann Prize, awarded to her in Israel by the International Council of Nurses. It was at that event she was dubbed "the most famous nurse in the world." What an event it was. I was there to witness it, along with my friend and colleague Kathleen Flynn. The night of the award ceremony we were helping her dress in her room. Earlier in the day she had sent her gown downstairs to be pressed. Later the bellman returned the dress; she insisted that he had forgotten the long scarf that went with it. He said that the scarf had not been sent with the dress. This exchange continued for a short time, each insisting on their "truth." Finally, she smiled that beguiling smile of hers and said in her most saccharine accent, "Well . . . either one of us could be wrong . . ." Then turning to us she said, "But I know it's not me!"

Kay and I began to search through the drawers in the room. Sure enough, the scarf had been lodged in one of the drawers. Virginia immediately wrote a note of apology to the bellman, included a tip, and had us deliver it to him. I have used those lines, "Either of us could be wrong, but I know it's not me," dozens of times since that occasion. Assertiveness, when used with humor and charm, is very persuasive!

I have learned much from this nurse who would discuss astrophysics and theology until the wee hours of the morning. Or the woman who was a gourmet cook. One night after dinner at her apartment, I was helping her clean up. Her refrigerator and cupboards were crammed full of outrageous delicacies, like crabmeat and pate and four different kinds of chocolate. I said to her, "Virginia, I've never see a refrigerator so full!" She replied, "Why, I get positively lonesome if my refrigerator doesn't look like that!" Humor, particularly when it is aimed at oneself, is so disarming.

In the fall of 1989 I invited Virginia Henderson to come to Seattle to be the keynote speaker at our organization's annual Nursing Congress. That year's event followed a painful and protracted nurses' strike that had played havoc with our organization just several weeks before. Healing was in order, and I could think of no one better equipped for the work. At age 91, Virginia agreed to come, and her breathless energy, warmth, wit, humor, charm, intelligence, and integrity were made to order. During the event that night, I took some liberties with a familiar Beatles' tune, rewrote the words, and dedicated it to Miss Henderson:

> And in my hour of darkness
> Virginia's standing next to me,
> Speaking words of wisdom,
> Let it be.

Almost seven years later, I asked a number of my colleagues who met her to reflect on that experience. Here's what they said:

Barbara Trehearne, RN, wrote:

> I had the opportunity to meet Virginia Henderson in 1989 when she came to our organization to speak at a nursing function that followed a nurses' strike. I was already very familiar with her work, but what impressed me the most was her style and a presence that is not often seen in our current health care environment. She was gracious but did not mince words about the state of nursing. She was witty and yet right on the mark in her observations. She clearly did not shy away from controversy and yet she never offended. In the end I was most touched by a personal gesture on her part. Already in her nineties, she had begun to give away her lifetime possessions. My gift from her was a beautiful green suit, vintage 1940s, with a braid trim she had stitched on herself. She was truly a memorable woman.

Mary Pat Thorpe, RN, wrote:

> Our organization was very privileged to have Ms. Henderson at our Nursing Congress as we were about to piece ourselves back together after a very painful and divisive labor strike. We came to that event wearing the whole gamut of emotions, ranging from fear to hostile indifference, to a sense of loss for collegial friendships that may never be regained. The banquet room itself was divided with certain corners or sections containing certain factions. We even had some rather elite members of the medical staff and administration observing and wondering how the evening would go.
>
> When someone mentions her name to me, I remember this wonderful healing lady, giving her all for us; then when the microphone was no longer in front of her, she lowered her head over her bouquet of red roses and took a little nap. What a privilege it was to have actually met her, and what a smile she brings to me today when I remember her.

KayC Mcmanemy, RN, wrote:

I attended the nursing function when Virginia Henderson spoke. I was extremely impressed. She was an extremely bright and visionary person who was able to express the true essence of nursing in a way that still makes sense even in today's world of technology and health care changes. Besides being a nursing scholar, she was a delightful person to listen to and learn from. Even though I did not know her on a personal level, I feel the loss of such a grand person in a time where nursing needs much strength from its leaders.

Nancy Milkowski, RN, wrote:

What impressed me the most about Virginia Henderson was her perseverance and ongoing concern for patients. Given her age and length of nursing service, she embraced change and kept her desire to care for the ill, to promote wellness and support throughout the patient's healing process.

Diane D'Ewart, RN, wrote:

While listening to Virginia Henderson I had the powerful and comforting sense of being in an historic presence. When she died, I put a copy of her definition of nursing on my bulletin board in my office. I sent a copy of the memorial remembrance to my mother, aunt, and sister, who are all RNs, and thought of my late grandmother, also an RN. Why? A sense of belonging to a very important group.

Carmen Suazo, RN, wrote:

When I listened to Virginia Henderson the night she was here, the word *endurance* comes to mind. Of course I had heard what she said before during my years as a student and as a registered nurse, but it was still relevant today. She made me feel grounded and connected.

Lori Bulger Potts, RN, wrote:

Miss Henderson seemed to be a matriarch, a symbol of healing in our environment when we needed nurturing. She seemed to understand the issues without taking sides or being judgmental. She was the quintessential nurse who provided a "shot in the arm."

Katherine Graham, RN, wrote:

Being with Virginia Henderson was an "awesome" experience. I felt humble in the presence of a nursing giant. I remembered my confidence and pride in being a public health nurse. She restored my faith in nursing.

Suzanne Boyle, RN, wrote:

When I was a master's student at the Yale School of Nursing, I was doing a presentation for faculty and students. My 2½-year-old daughter was throwing Kleenex wads from the balcony. Virginia Henderson spied her and invited her to her office. Virginia spent the next hour with her and fed her "sweetmeats." I was so touched by her humanity and warmth.

Writing this article was a labor of love for me. I am very proud to say that Virginia Henderson was my friend. But most of all, Virginia always reminded me how proud I am to be a nurse. She also made me realize why I believe that women should run the world.

My Great Aunt

Catherine M. Burdge, MSN, RN
Clinical Nurse Specialist
Yale-New Haven Hospital
New Haven, CT
Great niece of Virginia Henderson

A***s a child,*** I always knew Virginia as my great aunt first and as a nurse second. She was a wonderful aunt, so loving and giving. And she was a wonderful nurse for the same reasons and more. Little did I know that the influence that she had on me during my younger years would steer me toward the nursing profession that I so deeply love.

One of my first recollections of Virginia the nurse was when I was five years old. Virginia was the guest speaker at the capping ceremony at Columbia Presbyterian Hospital. My family decided to go and surprise her there. My memories of this event are wonderful; the lighting was dimmed as the nursing students lit their candles and received their caps. There was a mystical atmosphere around us. Then there was Virginia, larger than life to me, up at the podium speaking to the audience. How impressive she was! I was so proud in my own five-year-old way. The ceremony not only stayed with me as a remembrance of how grand nursing is, but also how grand Virginia the nurse was. At that age I could sense the excitement and the love that she had for the profession.

My mother is also a nurse, influenced as well by Virginia. During my younger years, I would dress up in my mother's nursing uniform, put on her cap and her pin, and pretend that I was a nurse. I remember walking around the house feeling so proud to wear the uniform. That is how my mother and father made me feel about nursing and I know that Virginia laid the foundation for that.

We spent summers at the family home down South where Virginia would also spend a good part of the summer. Many mornings we would sit around the dining room table after breakfast discussing many different topics and sharing important events in our lives. So many of these discussions would turn to nursing, her thoughts on the profession, and health care issues too. She was fascinating. She would hold forth on her opinions, taking every challenge dealt to her. She was my role model, even though I didn't realize it at the time. Virginia would share her experiences in different countries. She would tell us all about the nurses she visited and their hospitality. She was always so touched by it all. It was obvious how much everyone loved and appreciated Virginia the nurse as we did Virginia the aunt. It was an intriguing, challenging life that she lived, so exciting in every way.

Many of Virginia's close friends were nurses. We would visit them often in New York City and we would have a fabulous time together. They would talk about their work with such style, grace, and enthusiasm. They had wonderful lives, and so much of their lives revolved around nursing. It was a part of them, just as I think it is with so many of us.

As I grew up, I started to lean toward becoming a physician. I was pre-med for a time in college but decided that it really wasn't the way that I wanted to go. I steered toward the humanities, but was continually drawn back to health care. Virginia was patient. Little did I know how she was influencing me. She was setting the example. During this time she was receiving awards and giving lectures all over the world. When we could, my family and I would attend. She was so inspiring, and I was so proud of her. I was beginning to realize how significant Virginia's contributions to nursing really were.

When Virginia received her honorary degree at Yale University, my family and I spent the weekend with her. It was a turning point for me. I was captive to her every move and word. She was surrounded by nurses who were just as inspiring as she was. I was really understanding what the profession was all about. How thrilling it was! I left that weekend knowing that I wanted to be a nurse. I called Virginia and spoke with her about it. She was wonderful and so smart about it all. She didn't want me to base my decision on her. She wanted me to meet other nurses and spend time talking with them about the profession. She put me in contact with clinical as well as academic nurses, who kindly took the time to talk with me and share their experiences with me. My excitement grew.

Once I applied to nursing school, Virginia stepped back. She wanted me to be accepted for who I was, not for who she was. When I was accepted to nursing school, we certainly did celebrate! What fun it was to study her theories and achievements in nursing research. And I enjoyed sharing with my family the "inside story" on Virginia.

I have been a nurse for twelve years now, and I cannot imagine choosing any other career. Virginia, and my mother, gave this gift to me. For this I always will be eternally grateful. Not a day goes by when I don't think of Virginia in my practice. I use her basic needs framework with each patient, if not formally in writing, then in my mind. And her definition of nursing is the foundation of my practice. What an honor it is to carry on her beliefs and share them with patients as well as nursing and physician colleagues. And what an honor it has been to get to know my dear great aunt even better over the years. She will always be with me in so many ways.

On Civility

Judith B. Krauss, MSN, RN, FAAN
Dean and Professor
Yale University School of Nursing
New Haven, CT

W*e at Yale* were privileged to know Virginia Henderson as family. She lived and worked among us for the last 45 years of her life—arguably the most productive years of her career. For us, they were a veritable feast of the Henderson wit, charm, and wisdom. I first met Virginia in the fall of 1968, when I enrolled as a first-year graduate student in Yale's Psychiatric-Mental Health Nursing Program, so I knew her for 28 years. It was Virginia who taught me about civility—social civility and scholarly civility.

Over the course of nearly three decades, I was a liberal participant in the legendary Henderson dinner parties, crafted with care and elegance and usually designed to not only please the palate but to stretch the mind. Ever the Southern gentlewoman, Virginia Henderson was an exquisite cook. Her parties were meticulously planned, from the complicated menu, which took days to prepare, to the fine place settings and carefully arranged seating plans (always around small tables and never with one's partner), to the crowning glory—the chocolate desserts.

But most of her parties had a not-so-hidden agenda. I remember one that she gave in honor of Monsieur LeBoyer, whom she had met during her travels in France and whose birthing techniques involving water and low lighting captured her attention; so much so that she set about the uphill task of convincing the department of Obstetrics and Gynecology at the Yale School of Medicine to co-sponsor with the Yale School of Nursing a LeBoyer lecture. As you might imagine, LeBoyer's ideas were not widely embraced at Yale, where high technology, even with something as natural as the birth process, was king. When it became clear that the Medical School was not going to willingly cooperate, Virginia changed strategy and invited everyone to one of her elegant dinner parties. Believe me, when one was invited, one attended! Who do you imagine was the guest of honor? Who else but Monsieur LeBoyer, to be preceded, of course, by his lecture. One could not risk attending the party not having heard the lecture. Thus it was that the Yale School of Medicine collaborated with the School of Nursing on the controversial program. And, thus it was that Virginia Henderson, through the wise use of civility, once again succeeded in introducing important, pioneering, person-focused ideas related to the humanization of health care.

Civility suited Virginia Henderson and was a good fit with Yale. Civility reigned even during the most mundane phase of the *Nursing Studies Index* project, conducted at Yale. Virginia and her research assistants would stop for tea each afternoon and for sherry each Friday; served in a room with elegant carpet on the floor, fine paintings on the wall and a huge unsightly bin of IBM key sort cards in the middle of the carpet—tea with fine china and a silver tea set; sherry with crystal decanter and appropriate glassware; and conversation about nursing, the classics, the arts—elegant sustenance for an equally elegant mind.

Virginia was first and foremost an independent investigator and scholar. Although many mistakenly think she was once a Yale School of Nursing Dean, she never labored under any form of administrative constraint and was always free, in the classic sense of academic freedom, to pursue and express ideas. She was generous and enthusiastic by nature and interested in the ideas and perceptions of others. She was always able to see seeds of wisdom in colleagues' and students' minds, and she publicly and privately inspired, encouraged, and facilitated the blossoming of ideas into visions of leadership and improved patient care. She gave generously of her time to faculty and students alike and clearly shaped Yale's commitment to practice and the improvement of health care for all people. She regularly participated in the Issues Seminar with our first-year students until two years prior to her death.

Surely, her classical, elegant writing and speaking style, as well as her disdain for jargon, especially for nursing diagnosis, rubbed off on me. I think of Virginia Henderson as Aristotelian; that is, at once both intellectual and practical about the nature of things, like nursing and health care. She had the courage and self-confidence to be independent of thought, the humility or perhaps the good judgment to put title and earnings aside, and the generosity of spirit to encourage others to pursue ideas. On the other hand, she didn't hesitate to inform me if she thought my ideas were wrong, however interesting they might be. I always knew when I had struck a discordant chord with Virginia. She would materialize in my office doorway, dressed in a flowing skirt and one of her famous capes, carrying an umbrella and large black bag full to overflowing with her current papers and journal articles. She usually approached me with her Southern charm saying, "Now, honey, this is just my opinion . . ." or, "Do you have time for a visit with an old lady?" Old lady indeed! She was wise, but not old. One always emerged from such dialogues feeling renewed and relieved that she was willing to share her thoughts privately, colleague to colleague. One often emerged from such dialogues having changed one's mind about the issue at hand. Ah, civility!

To me, Virginia Henderson was a true scholar, teacher, and contemplative activist—a grace-filled humanist who always lit up a room. People always remarked about her eyes. There was the light of truth and curiosity behind those eyes. When I think of her in pure form, I think of love, passion, and virtue. She walked in balance on this earth, with one foot in the spiritual and one foot in the physical. She knew no barriers, attracted as she was to people and ideas of all persuasions. The values, ideas, styles, and colors that were the touchstones of her individual life were woven into the texture and substance of her ideas about nursing and health care. She was a good friend who traveled with many of us through seasons of our lives. In her own words, she "just kept on hoeing her cabbages." It has finally dawned on me that I'm one of those cabbages and it's my job to keep growing. To borrow a very well-known phrase, Virginia Henderson had the "strength, will, and knowledge" to pursue ideas with passion, conviction, and civility; and, those ideas, like the woman herself, remain forever young and forever relevant to nursing around the world. I am grateful to have known her and, more importantly, to have been influenced by her in ways I do not yet comprehend.

Part II
Scholarship

Collaboration in New England

Mary Ellen Doona, EdD, RN
Associate Professor
Boston College School of Nursing
Chestnut Hill, MA

T***he foliage would be at its peak*** each October as nurses and librarians arrived at the New England Center at the University of New Hampshire for the annual meeting of the New England Regional Council for Library Resources for Nursing (NERCLRN). Virginia A. Henderson, Mary L. Pekarski, and Mary Ann Garrigan would greet them. Then the trio would focus the group on the urgent task of facilitating nurses' access to information.

Each of the trio had a long history of helping nurses with their information needs. Each knew the time when nursing had no bibliographic tools and the only access to nursing's scholarly record consisted of the annual index to an individual periodical. The *American Journal of Nursing*, for example, published its index at the end of the year. Other indexes in the 1950s were homemade affairs that individual librarians created for their nursing patrons. Virginia A. Henderson confronted this situation firm in the conviction that nursing could not advance as a profession without orderly access to its literature. To further her mission, Henderson established an interdisciplinary coordinating council that in 1960 voted to call itself the Interagency Council on Library Resources for Nursing (ICLRN). Its purposes were to validate the inadequacy of library resources for nursing, recommend a national or international nursing index, and establish regional bodies for information gathering. It was from this effort that the NERCLRN had emerged.

Henderson spent eleven years finding nursing's fugitive literature starting with 1900 and ending with 1959. The magnificent *Nursing Studies Index* (NSI), which Henderson directed, appeared in four volumes (1963, 1966, 1970, and 1972). The NSI provided an annotated "guide to the analytical, historical and biographical aspects of the literature on nursing published in English" (Henderson, 1972, p. vii). The *Cumulative Index to the Nursing and Allied Health Literature* (CINAHL) was the first to take up Henderson's challenge and indexed nursing's literature from 1956 forward. The *International Nursing Index* (INI) followed and began its index with the nursing literature that started in 1966.

During those years of Henderson's heroic efforts, Mary Pekarski was creating a nursing library at Boston College. From its beginning in 1947, this library was unique in its commitment to nursing as a scholarly profession. Such excellence did not escape Virginia A. Henderson's perceptive eye. She already knew of Pekarski's collaboration with the Regional Medical Library in Boston, which through Pekarski's library had made resources available to Henderson. Henderson joined Pekarski at meetings with the Regional Medical Library. They spoke as one for nursing's information needs. Henderson said of her colleague, "Nursing owes a great debt to Mary L. Pekarski. As librarian of the Boston College nursing library, [Pekarski] presides over what I believe to be the best nursing library in this or any other country I have visited" (Henderson, 1985).

If Henderson began her relationship with Pekarski over their mutual commitment to library resources for nurses, she knew Mary Ann Garrigan from the time Garrigan was one of her students at Teachers College, Columbia University. Garrigan had many influential positions in nursing, but the pinnacle was being the founder, developer, and curator of the Nursing Archives at the Mugar Memorial Library at Boston University (BU), where the collection was officially recognized in March 1966. In July 1971, the Nursing Archives became the official repository for the papers of the American Journal of Nursing Company, and that September, the American Nurses Association added its papers to the expanding archives. In the same year Virginia Henderson selected the Nursing Archives at BU as the repository for all of her professional papers. The present inventory of her collection indicates that there are fifteen boxes of documents.

The current reawakening of nursing's interest in its past and its enduring service to humanity validates Garrigan's foresight. About Garrigan, Virginia Henderson said, ". . . her work as an archivist has been a beacon to nursing in this country where nurses have been singularly . . . [slow] in developing and preserving all sorts of scholarly resources" ("A tribute to . . .," 1986, p. 7). The Nursing Archives preserve nursing's memory and ensure that it will be accessible to nurses in the decades and centuries to come.

Henderson, Pekarski, and Garrigan were a formidable trio—a bibliographer, a librarian, and an archivist—each from a different New England academic institution. Alone and with one another they served nurses. Their happy and fecund collaboration initiated the first meeting at the University of New Hampshire (UNH). By the second year, the October NERCLRN meeting at UNH already was a not-to-be-missed date on the calendar. Far from the nursing's urgent world of action, and dazzled by nature's spectacular unleafing before the long cold New England winter, nurses addressed the question to librarians that had prompted the collaboration and originated the conference: "What are you doing for nurses?"

Together, Henderson, Pekarski, and Garrigan ensured that nurses would have access to the profession's literature. Individually each graced nursing with her excellence. The love and respect that Henderson, Pekarski, and Garrigan had for one another nurtured to full growth nurses' bibliographic access to their profession's literature. Their collaboration remains an exemplar.

References

A tribute to Mary Ann Garrigan. (1986). *Journal of Nursing History, 2*(2), 2-7.

Doona, M.E. (1984). N.E. Regional Council of Library Resources for Nursing. unpublished material.

Henderson, V. (1972). *Nursing studies index* (Vol. 1). Philadelphia: Lippincott.

Henderson, V.A. (1985, May 6). *A tribute to Mary L. Pekarski.* Massachusetts Association of Colleges of Nursing, Massachusetts Nurses Association and Massachusetts and Rhode Island League for Nursing Citizen Award for Nursing.

Tributes

Nancy Dickenson-Hazard, MSN, RN, FAAN
Executive Officer
Sigma Theta Tau International
Indianapolis, IN

V***irginia Henderson once said*** that her students would tell her, "Miss Henderson, if I haven't learned anything else, I have learned how to use the literature," to which she quickly replied, "You couldn't have paid me a greater compliment" (1991). Her strong belief in the power of literature to help nurses improve their practice was and remains today the perfect representation of Sigma Theta Tau International's mission to disseminate nursing knowledge. She stated this belief most eloquently in 1987 when she said, "When nurses' sensitivity to human needs (their intuition) is joined with the ability to find and use expert opinion, with the reported research and apply it to their practice, and when they themselves use the scientific method of investigation, there is no limit to the influence they might have on health care world wide" (1992, p. 4). It is no wonder then that in 1990, Sigma Theta Tau International named its unique electronic library in honor of Virginia Avenel Henderson, educator, humanitarian, and scholar.

In 1979, at Sigma Theta Tau International's twenty-fifth biennial convention in Seattle, Miss Henderson, along with Dr. Eleanor Herrmann and Dr. Anne Bavier, presented a resolution to the House of Delegates to promote and develop a national nursing library resource. With the unanimous passage of this resolution, development began on a library that would address the long-standing inadequacy of mechanisms to assist nurses in accessing their profession's research literature. Building a library that would serve as a repository of nursing research was a vision that the leadership of Sigma Theta Tau International shared with Miss Henderson.

Emulating what Miss Henderson regarded as her greatest contribution to nursing, the *Nursing Studies Index*, the new model would be an electronic storehouse of knowledge, structured on a research classification system. Through three editions, the classification system has evolved into *The Registry of Nursing Research*, a registry of nurse researchers, their studies, and the knowledge generated by their scientific inquiry.

It was the promise, the potential of what this international nursing library could do for the practice of nursing, that prompted Virginia Henderson in 1990 to allow her good name to be associated with it. According to Sigma Theta Tau International's then president, Dr. Billye Brown, "Virginia approved the concept of the 'Virginia Henderson Library' because of its future services to practicing nurses"(1990, p. 1). Miss Henderson believed this one-of-a-kind resource would assist practicing nurses in improving the delivery of health care by using the science of nursing. Sigma Theta Tau International believed no other person was more deserving of the honor of having an international library named after them than Virginia Henderson. She was beloved and distinguished across the globe for her extraordinary contributions to the profession.

Miss Henderson's permission to name the library in her honor was secured on December 5, 1990 in a formal signing ceremony at Yale University, New Haven, Connecticut. Dr. Billye Brown and then Executive Officer Nell J. Watts had traveled to New Haven to execute the signing. The contract between Virginia Henderson and Sigma Theta Tau International was witnessed by Judith B. Krauss, Dean of the Yale University School of Nursing, Dr. Linda A. Lewandowski, then president of Delta Mu chapter, and Dr. James A. Fain, Sigma Theta Tau International member. At the same time, Miss Henderson agreed to participate in the celebration of Sigma Theta Tau International's 75th Anniversary, which would occur in 1997, the same year that she would turn 100 years old. The prospect of a dual celebration was thrilling, and initial plans were set in motion to pay tribute to this beloved icon of nursing.

During the 1993-1995 biennium, the 75th Anniversary Committee, chaired by Dr. Juliann Sebastian, developed the concept of publishing a festschrift to celebrate Virginia Henderson. A relatively new concept to nursing, the festschrift was envisioned as a scholarly tribute to Miss Henderson in celebration of her hundredth birthday and Sigma Theta Tau International's 75th Anniversary through a collection of essays contributed by students, colleagues, family, and admirers. Dr. Eleanor K. Herrmann, friend and colleague of Miss Henderson, was invited to be the editor of the publication. The dream was on its way to reality.

The opportunity for my one brief, yet memorable encounter with Virginia Henderson came on Sunday, November 6, 1994 when Dr. Fay Bower, then president of Sigma Theta Tau International, and I visited Miss Henderson at her home in Connecticut. Dr. James Fain had made arrangements with Virginia through her dear friends, Florence and Henry Wald, for us to meet with Virginia to demonstrate the library's current capabilities and to ask her permission to publish the festschrift in her honor. While I had enjoyed the privilege of hearing her speak, or hold "conversations," as she was fond of saying on several occasions, going to her home for a private discourse felt much like I would imagine the excitement of meeting the Pope or head of state. Although Connecticut was our last stop on a travel junket, I could hardly wait to encounter Virginia. Armed with flowers, candy (Virginia did enjoy chocolates!), and a laptop computer and speakers, Jim Fain drove us from Providence, Rhode Island to Connecticut for our 11:00 AM appointment.

At the Gables in Guilford, Connecticut we were greeted by Henry Wald and escorted into Virginia's modest one-bedroom apartment, which was furnished with family furniture and accented with light cheery florals and lace. Florence was in the bedroom assisting Virginia with her dressing. As I scanned the room, a lifetime of greatness passed before me. Intermingled with photos of family and friends were memorabilia from all around the globe. Virginia had touched the lives of many, both in and out of nursing; expressions and recognition of their gratitude were obvious. She later told me she wasn't sure why there was "all the fuss" from people and that she had enjoyed her life.

Florence emerged from the bedroom alone and explained that Virginia would be with us momentarily as she was finishing her hair. She also explained that Virginia had slowed down quite a bit in the past months and was experiencing greater hearing difficulties. I had been told by others that Virginia had lost quite a bit of weight and her health was failing. So when Virginia walked out to greet us a few moments later, I was stunned by her youthful persona. She may have been 96, but she looked hearty and full of life. As she walked slowly but deliberately toward us, the sun came through the window and shrouded her, creating a soft, almost beatific appearance. Yes, she had lost weight, but it made her look much younger. Yes, she was slower, but her eyes were still bright and impish; and yes, she was hard of hearing, but she still said, "Please call me Virginia" to our greetings of Miss Henderson.

Once seated on her sofa, Virginia assumed her role as a Southern hostess, offering us mid-morning tea and not being content until we were all sipping and munching. We shared stories of growing up in the South and she told how these traditions of graciousness and hospitality had served her well over the course of her life and career. One story I remember in particular was how important she thought flowers were to an occasion and how she would go into New York City to purchase them for events at the Yale School of Nursing. She said she could always find a great selection at good prices; plus she liked to visit the busyness of the city. Seldom was she disappointed, except one time when all she could find were orange, red, and yellow flowers. She bought them, even though they weren't what she had in mind, and it turned out to be her most cheerful bouquet ever!

During the course of the next hour, we conversed about the breadth of her work in nursing, which she summed up as, "I was just doing what I liked doing;" about her many honorary degrees and awards, to which she concluded she had so many now she couldn't remember them all individually but was grateful for them; and about her writings, which she said was "just the right thing to do at the time." She was so humble, so unassuming that I wondered if she understood how truly in awe and appreciative we in nursing were of her works and contributions. When I asked her she just smiled and said, "Thank you." We talked about her importance to Sigma Theta Tau International and the progress of the Virginia Henderson International Nursing Library. She told me she had been pleased to have the library named after her and that she enjoyed reading *Reflections*, a copy of which was on her coffee table.

Then we brought out the laptop computer to show her the CD ROM library demonstration developed by Dr. Betsy Weiner and her colleagues at the University of Cincinnati. While Virginia could readily see the screen of the laptop, hearing was a challenge for her. So with Fay Bower holding a speaker to her right ear and Jim Fain holding one to her left ear, she experienced the electronic tour of the library, the audiovisual image of herself speaking about the importance of literature to the practice of nursing, and an abbreviated sample search of the literature on women and cancer. She watched with great enthusiasm and intensity and when I asked if she wanted to see it again, she immediately said "Oh, yes." She was clearly pleased to see her legacy to nursing expressed in this way. "I never imagined this," she said when she saw that her dream of literature access to practicing nurses was now instantaneous and global. Her pride and even amazement were felt by all in the room.

Finally when I asked her permission to publish the festschrift in honor of her hundredth birthday, she replied, with that infamous twinkle in her eyes, "Why would you want to do that?" But as she was signing the agreement she looked at me and said, "This is wonderful, thank you."

All too soon it was time to leave. As she rose from the couch, Virginia opened her arms for an embrace and expressed her appreciation for our coming. She said, "I am always honored by visitors from Sigma Theta Tau." It was hard for me to turn and leave because once again Virginia Henderson had touched a life. Her graciousness, her wisdom, her humility, and her wit will be forever emblazoned in my heart and mind.

I was saddened because we on earth could not witness Virginia's receiving this tribute. This demonstration of nursing's respect and appreciation of Virginia is small compared to what she gave us. But her delight would be apparent if she were here. And we should all envision those blue eyes twinkling now as she looks down on us. Why, you asked, Virginia, did we want to do this festschrift, this tribute to your life and works? The answer is very simple: we love you, we admire you, we thank you for sharing your life with us.

References

Goldsmith, J. (1994). *Chronology of development of a nursing research library: The Virginia Henderson International Nursing Library.* Unpublished manuscript. Sigma Theta Tau International, Indianapolis, Indiana.

Graves, J.R. (1997). The Virginia Henderson International Nursing Library: Resource for nurse administrators. *Nursing Administration Quarterly, 21*(3), 76-83.

Halamandaris, V. (1988). A tribute to Virginia Henderson: The first lady of nursing. *Caring, 7*(10), 56-65.

Henderson, V., Herrmann, E., & Bavier, A. (1979). *Resolution: Nursing library services—national development.* 25th Biennial Convention, Sigma Theta Tau International, Seattle, Washington. Sigma Theta Tau International, Indianapolis, Indiana.

International nursing library named in honor of Virginia Henderson. (1990). *Reflections, 16*(4), 1.

Virginia Henderson. (1991, Nov.). Transcription of taped conversation at Sigma Theta Tau International 31st Biennial Convention, Tampa, Florida. Sigma Theta Tau International, Indianapolis, Indiana.

Virginia Henderson, RN—humanitarian and scholar. (1992). *Reflections, 18*(1), 4-5.

Three Questions

Nettie Birnbach, EdD, RN, FAAN
Boca Raton, FL;
Professor Emeritus
Health Science Center at Brooklyn
State University of New York
Brooklyn, NY

Virginia Henderson's definition of nursing had a profound effect on my professional life, beginning with my student days when the fourth edition (1939) of the Harmer and Henderson *Principles and Practice of Nursing* was a required textbook in the school of nursing I attended. Because of my enormous respect for the printed word, I avoided underlining or highlighting passages in my books, with one exception—the Henderson definition. With its direct approach, easily understood language, and emphasis on the patient/nurse relationship, the definition served as a guide for my practice as both clinician and educator. Students were consistently impressed by its simplicity and underlying wisdom. In reviewing the definition, I find it as relevant today as it has been throughout my career:

> Nursing may be defined as that service to the individual that helps him to attain or maintain a healthy state of mind or body, or, where a return to health is not possible, the relief of pain and discomfort.

In 1982, I was privileged to hear Miss Henderson when she spoke at a meeting of the Society for Nursing History held at Teachers College, Columbia University in New York. During her presentation, she discussed three questions that nursing students (or graduate nurses) could use in order to determine their patient's perception of the care rendered:

> What did I do that helped you?
> What did I do that didn't help you?
> What did I not think of that might have helped you?

The questions were so compelling that I began to use them with both undergraduate and graduate students as a tool for examining the quality of nursing practice. The questions were particularly useful for a group of graduate students conducting research related to the nursing care of patients with AIDS. The answers to the questions frequently conflicted with the way the nurses perceived their practice and led to increased insight.

Virginia Henderson was the recipient of numerous awards during her long and productive lifetime. In 1988, I was present when she received a Special Citation of Honor from the American Nurses Association at its convention in Louisville, Kentucky. I was seated near her and took advantage of the opportunity to express my ongoing appreciation for the fourth edition of *The Principles and Practice of Nursing.* Miss Henderson smiled, thanked me, and then commented, "You should get the sixth edition, it's much better."

A Canadian Perspective

JANET C. ROSS KERR, PHD, RN
Professor, Faculty of Nursing
University of Alberta
Edmonton, Alberta, Canada

Like many other Canadian nursing students who were my contemporaries, my introduction to Virginia Henderson occurred when I was a first year student. I learned about her from my professor of nursing and her book entitled *Principles and Practice of Nursing*. This text provided me with my first glimpse of what nursing was really about, and its pages became worn during that first year. However, it remained an important reference throughout my student days. Although the authors were Bertha Harmer and Virginia Henderson, I learned much later from Virginia Henderson herself that she was actually the sole author of the book. Following Bertha Harmer's death in 1934, the publisher had approached Miss Henderson and asked her to assume authorship of the book. By the time I was a beginning student of nursing, Virginia Henderson had been its sole author for almost a quarter of a century! The fundamental values that characterized the substance of the book were those that Virginia Henderson believed in deeply and continued to articulate throughout the remainder of her career. Hers was a career that continued long after retirement, for she remained active and committed to her profession until her death.

Virginia Henderson believed deeply in the dignity and worth of the individual and in the importance of respect for the person. Her personal warmth and graciousness and the respect she showed to others provided a wonderful example of the qualities she expected nurses to show to their patients. An early role model of a nursing scholar, she pursued excellence and scholarship in nursing at an early stage of the development of the profession. Her work to develop the *Nursing Studies Index* was seminal and provided a guide to scholarly work in nursing from 1900 onwards. Yet she bore no truck with nursing jargon and with using oblique, abstract, and difficult language to express what could be said much more simply. She always had difficulty with the concept of the nursing process and did not hesitate to say so and to explain the reasons for her view. Clearly Miss Henderson did not approve of "jumping on bandwagons" and was not impressed by flowery language. She encouraged nurses to think and speak for themselves and not to be influenced and driven by the latest fashion in the profession.

Nursing came alive for me from the outset of my student experience, and it was illuminated by Virginia Henderson. I learned a great deal about this woman and her ideas from the nursing professor who taught my first course in nursing. Jean Wilson, a faculty member at the University of Toronto, herself both an outstanding teacher and a nurse committed to the dignity and respect for patients. It was she who communicated to me and my classmates the nature and substance of nursing as reflected in the ideas of Virginia Henderson, and her respect and admiration for Miss Henderson came through clearly. To this day I associate the concepts of caring and comfort fundamental to nursing practice with the picture of Virginia Henderson at this early stage of my career in nursing. Later in my career, I realized what a profound effect Virginia Henderson had on nurses across the broad spectrum of roles in the profession. My professor had shared her respect and admiration for Miss Henderson's ideas and values with many others.

As I continued in the field and took on a teaching role, I extended my understanding of Virginia Henderson's work as I read *The Nature of Nursing* and explored her compilation of nursing studies. I began to take a more detailed look at the basis of her work. When I returned to graduate school, first for a master's degree, then for a PhD, I gained a new understanding of Virginia Henderson's scholarly work as I read it with more depth of understanding than previously. At that point, I became more involved in professional service activities than ever before. I eventually found myself in the position as president of the provincial professional association, the Alberta Association of Registered Nurses, and a member of the Board of Directors of the Canadian Nurses Association. The group of nurse volunteers who were my colleagues on these boards at the time came from all areas of practice, education, and research and they shared my admiration and respect for Virginia Henderson. Subsequently, our provincial professional organization decided to confer an honorary membership upon her. We invited her to be a keynote speaker for our annual convention, but were disappointed when she was unable to come at the last minute because of ill health. When Dr. Margaretta Styles agreed to step in at the eleventh hour and deliver a keynote address for us, she said that she did so with great humility because she found the very idea of serving as the replacement for Virginia Henderson both remarkable and daunting!

I had my first opportunity to meet Virginia Henderson in 1981 at the International Council of Nurses meeting in Los Angeles. A colleague of mine, Dr. Shirley Stinson, who corresponded regularly with Miss Henderson, invited her to a luncheon in her hotel room and invited me along with four or five others to join her. This was a momentous occasion for me and I am sure it was for the others, all of whom held this woman in esteem, if not awe! Miss Henderson's conversation was very entertaining, and she spoke easily and readily of her experiences in nursing. She talked of her concerns in relation to nursing at the time. She asserted that patients needed to be treated as individuals with more care and concern than she believed to be the norm at the time. She told of a recent occasion when she and her sister (I believe she said it was her sister, but as some time has passed I cannot be certain of this) had recently visited a friend in the hospital who was ready for discharge. When the friend was ready to leave, no one arrived to assist, so Virginia and her sister picked up the flower arrangements, suitcase, and other belongings and started down the hall as an entourage of three making their way to the elevator with all of the baggage. When they got to the desk, there were several nurses sitting around it who looked up, smiled, and proceeded to wave good-bye to them! The irony of this situation was not lost on Virginia Henderson, nor on those of us to whom she recounted the incident!

I was struck at the time by how perceptive Miss Henderson was about a whole range of issues in nursing past and present. True to form, Virginia Henderson did not hesitate to speak her mind on matters of concern to her, and she said whatever she had to say quite simply and directly. It seems to me that her powerful voice for nursing has stemmed from her intellect, her understanding of people, and her ability to articulate her views in a clear and straightforward manner. I was fortunate to hear Virginia Henderson speak on a number of other occasions (Sigma Theta Tau conferences and at the ICN in Tel Aviv), and each time I was again struck by the simplicity and substance of her message. However, I will always treasure the opportunity to have met and talked with her personally at the informal luncheon in the company of a small group of friends and colleagues, for it was a truly wonderful occasion.

The Search for Meaning in Life

Rev. William E. Bliss, MDiv
Stony Creek, CT;
Pastor Emeritus
First Congregational Church of Derby, CT

M*y wife Ann and I* were friends of Virginia Henderson from 1970 to the very peaceful final hour of her life when I was privileged to give her Holy Communion and final prayers.

One of the axioms of good manners is never to discuss religion or politics in polite society, so as not to offend. I remember Virginia fondly as a paragon of polite good manners who could render any difference of opinion with utmost charm and civility.

She undertook to discuss religion in her chapter "Worship" in *Principles and Practice of Nursing* (Henderson & Nite, 1978) in an age of heightened quest for spirituality and disdain for sectarian doctrine. This chapter remains for me a timely work of genius that ought to be required reading, not only for nurses and health care professionals, but for all teachers, lawyers, clergy, and businessmen and women in every field of endeavor.

It was typical of Virginia not only to have the intellectual grasp of a subject as complex and controversial as the religions of the world, but also to have great respect for other people's faiths and beliefs. Thus she was able to write a brilliant 42-page summary of nine major religions without slight or offense to anyone.

The power of her intellect is evident in the succinct depth and breadth with which she treats each religion, capturing the fine points *and* the spiritual essence of each—no mean feat as anyone knows who has ever labored over a religious treatise.

Moreover, Virginia understood and valued the goodness in other people. Her chapter begins, "It seems to be a human characteristic to believe, or want to believe, that there is a beneficent purpose in life and that there is a divine spark in man. The search for the good, the beautiful, the perfect, or the divine is what most distinguishes man from animals."

Virginia's own good health and long life support her statement that "good health seems to be dependent upon the belief that life has meaning or a 'good' purpose and upon behavior that is consistent with this meaning, this purpose, or value system." This is an apt description of her own life put to such good purpose.

It was one of Virginia Henderson's gifts to value the uniqueness of every individual and therefore to understand that there are as many religions in the world as there are people. It is hard to question the statement that "even the most devout or orthodox subscribers to a religious faith make their own interpretations or adaptions."

"It would seem if people are to be viewed whole by any health worker, their moral, ethical, spiritual, and religious values cannot be ignored . . . Religious beliefs, ethical concepts, moral values, or the meaning of life lie at the roots of each personality." She took the position that all illness has emotional and physical components, and that there is no health service that does not have a spiritual aspect. Her definitive and comprehensive views of nursing care are based in these religious beliefs.

One might ask how her endorsement of religious values speaks to people who seem to have no religious interest. Virginia answered this as follows: ". . . each person is unique. He or she develops a particular combination of beliefs, hopes, and fears derived from intuition, [from] what has been taught by parents and authority figures, and [from] what has been learned from experience. Even professed atheists hold some beliefs that have a religious origin—beliefs that hark back to the early teaching of authority figures."

Never pious, Virginia embodied the best of religious precepts. Hers was a spirituality better done than said. For me, she possessed the:

- wisdom of a Rabbi
- compassion of a Buddhist
- righteousness of a Muslim
- nonmaterialism of a Hindu
- goodness of a Christian Saint

Reference

Henderson, V., & Nite, G. (1978). *Principles and Practice of Nursing* (6th ed.). (pp. 1018-1060). New York: Macmillan.

A Physician's View

Morris A. Wessel, MD
Clinical Professor of Pediatrics
Yale University School of Medicine
New Haven, CT

I *experienced a sense of joy* whenever I had the good fortune to visit with Virginia Henderson. Whether these meetings occurred on the street, in the Yale School of Nursing, in the Yale Medical Library, or at a dinner party, her deep concern for all human beings always was apparent. She possessed a unique ability to communicate her firm belief that an understanding of human behavior and relationships was vitally important for nurses and physicians as they cared for patients. She stimulated all who met her to consider how one might improve ways of dealing with patients and family members as one provided professional service.

When I examined the sixth edition of *Principles and Practice of Nursing,* which she and Gladys Nite published in 1978, I was impressed with the strong emphasis that nurses and doctors can serve patients most effectively when they are aware of the life experiences, cultural background, and religious orientation of their patients.

Virginia Henderson in her chapters emphasizes that nurses, and doctors too, who have a continuing relationship can provide important continuous support for patients and family members. She suggests that the healing relationship offered by a nurse or doctor is enhanced when patients are encouraged to share how they conceive the meaning of their current health crisis or illness in terms of their beliefs and convictions. A nurse's or physician's presence and willingness to listen and comprehend the patient's and family's outlook often strengthen the healing process, no matter what the outcome of the illness. This relationship can exist whether the contact occurs in an office, community clinic, hospital, hospice, home, school, or industrial plant.

In order to help caregivers understand these factors, Virginia Henderson discussed various religious beliefs that often determine the manner in which a patient copes with illness or injury. Whatever a nurse's or physician's personal, cultural, and religious experiences may be, she believed that the ability to serve a patient and family members is vastly improved when one is aware of a patient's personal orientation. Even though a caregiver's personal beliefs may differ from those of a patient, she believed it important to comprehend and respect each patient's way of dealing with life at this difficult moment.

Another important role emphasized in this text is that of the nurse as a primary caretaker. This description was written in 1977 early in the conceptualization of the important role of nurse practitioners. I wonder if Virginia Henderson realized how prophetic she was in delineating this role, which now, twenty years later, assumes increasing importance in society. A health care professional must be easily accessible to a patient and family members and be ready to arrange for specialized consultation and laboratory studies while maintaining on ongoing relationship. A primary nurse practitioner or physician who assumes this role aids a patient and the family members obtain various consultation and laboratory studies and assists the patient through the complicated pathways that often obstruct appropriate consultation. A nurse's continued relationship with the patient and family offers ongoing support and is an important therapeutic force for patients and family members during this process. This role is of great importance currently with the rapid development of managed care as a predominant force in health care in this country.

The final chapter by Virginia Henderson and Florence Wald, prepared in the early days of the movement, considers ways of increasing recognition of how best to meet the needs of patients and family members during the terminal phase of life. The authors recognized the challenges nurses face while serving patients and families at that moment. The discussion presents the historical background of how the realization of this human need rose to prominence and emphasizes that family members also need help and support as they anticipate the loss of a loved one and during bereavement. The inclusion of this chapter indicates again Virginia Henderson's extensive conceptualization of the extent and importance of nurses in caring for patients.

A nurse caring for a patient with a terminal illness is in a unique position to help the patient not only with discomfort and physical needs, but also with adaptation to this difficult phase of life. Virginia Henderson and Florence Wald stressed that as one supports patients and families at these difficult moments, nurses, and doctors too, need to consider their own attitudes and feelings at such critical moments.

Virginia Henderson's diverse activities in the field of nursing education stimulated health personnel to work diligently in the pattern she so ably portrayed in her writings and activities. Those of us who knew her are grateful for her passion, her ideas, her clarity about her convictions, and her love for fellow human beings. Her life provides a rich heritage for all of us. The challenge is for us to carry on in the manner she so ably portrayed during her lifetime.

Point of Entry

Rhea C. Sanford, MSN, RN
Clinical Nurse Specialist
John Dempsey Hospital
University of Connecticut Health Center
Farmington, CT

M***y entry into nursing*** was through a combined basic professional nursing and graduate specialization program designed for college graduates at the Yale University School of Nursing. The move from basic preparation content to advanced practice content was rapid. My area of clinical concentration was surgical nursing. Rotation through a variety of surgical subspecialties was challenging, but it was made easier by the application of Virginia Henderson's definition of nursing and her framework of basic needs. Her framework afforded me a point of entry to patient care, a point from which I knew I could completely collaborate with patients in formulating and assisting their need for nursing services. Regardless of whether the surgical service was peripheral, vascular, cardiac, or general surgery, patients all had the same basic needs and consequent common problems when those needs were not being met.

After completing my master's degree, I took a position as a clinical nurse specialist for medical-surgical nursing at a university teaching hospital. My "specialty" became the breadth of medical-surgical nursing specialties encompassed under that umbrella. Surgical specialties included general surgery; orthopedics; neurosurgery; ear, nose, and throat; and gynecological oncology. The medical unit admitted patients from cardiology, pulmonary, nephrology, infectious disease, neurology, and geriatrics. My point of entry to understanding the nursing care issues of this diverse population of patients was, again, basic needs and common problems. Recognition of areas of common concern was a continuous focus for me during the first six months in my job. During that time, an experience with a new staff nurse helped me recognize the need to incorporate Miss Henderson's theory even more fully into my practice.

One morning after shift report, I discovered that the new graduate sitting next to me had not moved. Other staff members had left the report room to start their work day, but she was literally frozen in her chair. She explained that she did not know the pathology of all the disease states represented in her assignment; she had not had the experience of caring for all these patient populations as a student; she did not think she could provide care without having time to look up diagnoses and read about each condition. Together we reviewed her patient assignment, and from the perspective of basic needs and common problems, developed a plan of care for each patient. As the shift progressed, she presented a very different picture than the immobilized young woman I had seen at the end of the morning report. Application of Miss Henderson's basic needs had afforded this new nurse a point of entry to care. It was clear to me after that encounter that basic needs and common problems would be an especially effective framework for orienting new staff nurses who were expected to care for such a diverse population of patients.

A medical-surgical orientation program was subsequently developed according to Miss Henderson's basic care activities and the common problems associated with the patient populations served. Henderson's three-phase approach for nursing education was the framework for orientation content. The first phase was designed to assist the nurse in acquiring competence in helping the patient perform the fourteen functions delineated as basic nursing care. Phase two asked the nurse to consider problems common to many patients, regardless of their medical diagnoses, that may interfere with basic needs being met. The last phase placed these common problems within the context of a specific disease.

Nurses in this orientation program can quickly demonstrate the skills described in Henderson's first phase of education. Consequently, initial didactic content is offered with a focus on Henderson's second phase of education, common problems. Early classes focus on problems with oxygenation, immobility, disturbances in nutrition, changes in usual elimination patterns, infection, pain that can prevent necessary sleep and rest, and learning needs of patients and their families. Later in the orientation process, classes focus on Henderson's third phase, specific disease processes and how they effect the experience of illness and recovery. Care of the patient undergoing joint replacement, radical neck dissection, or bowel diversion is reviewed for surgical nursing staff. Disease-specific nursing care for patients with myocardial infarction, lung disease, and renal failure represents class content for those on the medical unit.

Henderson's phases of education nicely complement the learning needs of a new graduate working with a diversified group of patients. The presentation of content also addresses two important outcomes that need to occur during the orientation process: patients' need to receive necessary care, and the new staff nurse's need to feel that he or she is practicing safely and moving toward the specificity of care demonstrated by more senior nursing staff. The initial concentration on problems common to all medical-surgical patients allows new graduates the time to establish a sense of competence in skill areas that will be the foundation of their daily nursing care. It provides a framework around which the new nurse can plan care and evaluate patient outcomes. The transition to content specific to specialty areas is accomplished as nurses begin to discern and integrate the differences in presentation and resolution of patient symptoms depending on the pathophysiology and treatment of different disease stages. Progression in this transition is facilitated by Henderson's clarity of purpose for nursing—to assist patients in fulfilling their basic needs.

A new area of responsibility for me is the implementation of case management across the care continuum, a move beyond my previous boundary of acute care. There are a number of definitions of the case management process, but regardless of definition, the question driving the process is the same: what needs to be done by health care providers to bring to patients the necessary strength, skill, or knowledge so that they can maintain optimal health and be maximally independent in their care? Assessment of basic needs and functional ability are integral to the case management approach to care delivery. As I prepare for this broader scope of practice, I continue to rely on Miss Henderson's definition and theory of nursing, not just as a point of entry, but as a framework within which I can continue to appropriately define and meet patients' needs.

Applied Philosophy

Adele W. Pike, MSN, RN
Community Health Nurse
Visiting Nurse Association of Boston
Boston, MA

My ***first exposure*** to Miss Henderson's thoughts about nursing came in the summer of 1981. I had decided to change careers and enter nursing, and was excited about starting the Three Year Program for Non-Nurse College Graduates at the Yale School of Nursing in the Fall. Over the summer I received a suggested reading list for incoming students. Among the suggestions was Henderson and Nite's *Principles and Practice of Nursing*. I dutifully ordered it from my local bookstore, never expecting anything like the gray-covered tome I received.

I made a valiant attempt to get through the first chapters of *Principles and Practice* that summer, but it did not hold my attention. With little or no understanding of what nursing was, I found the text thick and seemingly outdated. I groaned at the prospect that this was the basis of the curriculum for my upcoming nursing education.

My first weeks at Yale were largely spent reading numerous chapters of Miss Henderson's text assigned by the faculty. The readings were considerably easier when accompanied by class discussion and faculty guidance, but I remained skeptical. Then one day in mid-October (I think), Miss Henderson was a guest in our class. I have no recollection of what I had expected her to be like, only that I was captivated by this diminutive lady with wonderful white hair who spoke of nursing with great love and respect and clarity and wisdom. Her conceptualization of what it means to be a nurse captured my imagination that afternoon and has influenced my practice and learning ever since.

Needless to say, the pages of my copy of *Principles and Practice* are now well worn; many have the corner folded back so that I can find certain sections more easily. There is a bookmark at the location of her definition of nursing and list of basic human needs that nurses attend to. There is also a bookmark noting the page of her recipe for milk and molasses enemas—a very effective intervention when needed; I have been unable to find instructions for it anywhere else.

Miss Henderson, through her writings and spoken words, helped me not only to apprehend what it means to be a nurse, but also to be able to articulate that meaning to nonnurses. Having been exposed to her teachings from the moment my socialization to nursing began, I have seldom experienced confusion about nurses' role or contribution to patient care; I have never doubted that nurses have a unique area of wisdom and skill and that they are full-fledged members of the health care team. The professional self-concept she inspired has allowed me to build collaborative relationships with physicians and other caregivers that contribute to more sensitive and effective patient care.

I had known that Miss Henderson's health had been failing over the past few years and that she had recently moved to an inpatient hospice. But even still when I received the message last March that she had died, I was unsteadied. "How are we going to keep alive her work and her teachings without her presence?" was my immediate reaction. It was a question I asked in sadness and in deep gratitude. The next morning at work I shared the news of Miss Henderson's death, fully expecting (and wanting) to share stories of how she had influenced practice with my nurse colleagues. To my surprise, none of them knew who she was. The idea that nurses had never been enriched by her work saddened and unsteadied me even more.

In my sadness and apprehension that morning I decided that the best way to honor Miss Henderson's life was to take care of patients the way she had taught me to. My first patient was an elderly widower whom I've known for over two years. He's a sad man who misses his wife intensely. I see him because he has marked lower extremity weakness and COPD. When I got to his home that morning, he was up in his wheelchair trying to fix his breakfast. He was quite short of breath and was having a tough time just getting milk and juice out of the refrigerator.

I listened to his lungs and heard wheezing throughout, his heart rate was up a bit, and he seemed a bit more anxious than usual. I thought to myself, as I always do in caring for patients, how can I best help this man meet his basic needs? I suggested that he wait on breakfast until I could help him breathe a bit better. He agreed, and I helped him back into bed. I then performed chest percussion to his posterior lung fields and helped him deep breath and cough. He was able to bring up a fair amount of sputum and his work of breathing started to ease. I then washed his back and rubbed lotion on it, partly to provide him some comfort and partly to give him a rest period to recover from the pulmonary toilet. After he had rested I assisted him back into his wheelchair and asked if he wanted to brush his teeth while I fixed his breakfast.

He washed himself up a bit while I made him some instant oatmeal and coffee and poured a glass of orange juice. I sat at the table as he ate and chatted with him as I did my charting. We didn't talk about anything of great significance. I think we discussed the upcoming start of the baseball season. He finished his breakfast and I my progress note. He was breathing much easier and seemed less anxious. He told me he felt strong enough to wash up his dishes and thanked me for my visit.

This all seems so simple, so mundane; to the unenlightened it might even seem unskilled, intuitive. But to me it was the careful application of Miss Henderson's principles of nursing: helping this man meet those basic needs that he could not meet unaided and doing so in a way that fostered his independence and rehabilitation. Knowing that her teaching and philosophy of nursing were secure in my practice steadied me that day last March and taught me that the finest way to honor and keep alive her work is to keep practicing in accordance with her ideas about what nursing is and can be.

Recollections

Mildred L. Montag, EdD, RN, FAAN
Garden City, NY;
Professor Emeritus
Teachers College, Columbia University
New York, NY
Former student of Virginia Henderson at
Teachers College, Columbia University

M*y first contact* with Virginia was in the fall of 1937 when I registered for her course in the study of nursing procedures at Teachers College, Columbia University. The course included an intensive review of how nursing procedures were carried out with resulting study of how they could be improved. Having been teaching a first course in nursing, this was of interest to me. Although research was not on everyone's tongue at that time, we were really doing research. As one example, three other students and I selected giving nursing care —e.g., bed bath—to a patient in an oxygen tent.

Virginia secured an oxygen tent and a supply of oxygen, and we tried many approaches to giving the care and keeping the oxygen concentration at the prescribed level. We eventually outlined an acceptable procedure on the basis of our findings. An article on this "research" was published in the *American Journal of Nursing* (Hawthorne, Henderson, Montag, and Warfield, 1938). I do not recall Virginia using the word *research.* Perhaps we were ahead of our time. This course, which ran for two semesters, greatly influenced my teaching of nursing.

It was probably this course that was responsible for my assisting Virginia in her revision of Harmer's *Principles and Practice of Nursing.* Virginia always referred to her as "Miss Harmer." One thing of interest to me was that Virginia paid for all of the preparation of the manuscript, including the photographs, while a percentage of the royalties went to the Harmer estate. My participation in the manuscript, including writing four chapters, was an invaluable experience for me.

My professional contacts with Virginia continued while I was teaching at St. Luke's Hospital School of Nursing. Virginia's students observed my classes, and two of her students served as interns with me for one year.

My social contacts continued until Virginia left New York. Thereafter it was by irregular correspondence, but we never lost touch. Two recollections of the social contact are rather typical. Virginia's sisters were engaged in producing jams, jellies, and mustard, among other things, presumably from family recipes, for they had the names of "Miss ——'s mustard," etc. Virginia became their representative; I know because I bought them from her. The other recollection relates to her passion for chocolate. A friend and I were invited to Virginia's for dinner and when we entered her apartment the odor of burnt chocolate was very evident. At that time, Rose Marie French Chocolate was her choice. In melting it, it had burned. Not to be daunted, she simply melted more chocolate and the dessert was ice cream with hot chocolate sauce. After dinner Virginia produced a guitar and proceeded to entertain us by singing Southern songs.

My last contact with Virginia was when she spoke at the annual meeting of the three Sigma Theta Tau chapters on Long Island. She announced that she no longer wrote speeches but she agreed to answer questions, which she did. She was her usual entertaining but thoughtful self. Listening to her I thought she had the right idea. At dinner she related to me how the nice young man who drove her would not take a tip because she was such a nice lady. I suspect she entertained him all the way from New Haven.

Virginia was to me a teacher and a colleague, but most of all a very good friend, one whose influence was lasting.

Reference

Hawthorne, M., Henderson, V., Montag, M., & Warfield, M. (1938). Oxygen therapy: A study in some nursing aspects of the operation of an oxygen tent. *American Journal of Nursing, 38*(11), 1203-1216.

Legacy: Defining Nursing

Angela Barron McBride, PhD, RN, FAAN
Distinguished Professor and Dean
Indiana University School of Nursing
Indianapolis, IN
President (1987-89) Sigma Theta Tau

My ***thoughts on Virginia Henderson's rich legacy*** will focus on her elegant definition of nursing and my own changing perceptions of its meaning over the years, in order to make the case that it is particularly relevant at this point in time, and not just historically interesting. In case anyone needs to be reminded of her definition, it reads:

> Nursing is primarily helping people (sick or well) in the performance of those activities contributing to health, or its recovery (or to a peaceful death) that they would perform unaided if they had the necessary strength, will, or knowledge. It is likewise the unique contribuition of nursing to help people to be independent of such assistance as soon as possible. (Henderson, 1978, p. 34)

When I first read this definition in 1960 during my baccalaureate education, it was as the working definition of nursing adopted by the International Council of Nurses, something to be accorded respect because it described the thinking of an important professional organization. To the extent that I thought about it much at that time, I regarded the definition as an operational statement of what caregiving was about—practical, health oriented, and patient focused. At this stage of my career development, my stance was primarily one of acceptance; I was prepared to accept the conceptualization of my field's elders.

By the 1970s, I was no longer as accepting of what elders had to say, as I was deeply affected by the rethinking of the women's movement (McBride, 1976). I began analyzing Henderson's definition with a feminist perspective and was critical. The definition was so broad and seemingly without boundaries that I judged it to be part of women's basic problem, being held responsible for everything but not being acknowledged as expert in any area. Helping individuals do for themselves what they would do unaided, if they knew what to do, sounded like common sense to me and consequently likely to be dismissed as not counting for much. Though I was quick to note that sense is not common and that it takes years of education and experience to be able to address a broad range of needs effectively, I feared that such a definition of nursing reinforced stereotyped thinking. For example, that view seemed to urge nurses to be much like that mythic creature, the good mother, who does what is needed—fills in the spaces—always mindful that her real job is to no longer be needed. And if she has needs herself, they are regarded as character flaws, because her person is not supposed to intrude on the nurse-patient relationship but only be an instrument in service to the client. Such an impossible job description struck me as destined to make nurses feel like failures more times than not, because they were regularly likely to fall short of such idealized behavior.

I read into Henderson's definition of nursing much that my newfound feminist sensibility railed against—society's expecting women to be selfless in doing thankless work. Women's work (and nursing was very much regarded then as women's work) was expected to accomplish the extraordinary—contribute to health by knowing something about everything and having the strength of body and mind to meet any challenges—but there was every likelihood that these feats of mastery would be dismissed as nothing more than attending to the basics once the needs had been met.

It is important to note that Henderson was not unmindful that her words could be so construed:

> This concept of the nurse as a substitute for what patients lack to make them "complete," "whole," or "independent," be it the lack of physical strength, will, or knowledge, may seem limited to some who read this. The more one thinks about it, however, the more complex is the nurse's function, as so defined. Think how rarely one sees independence, completeness, or wholeness of mind and body! . . . If, then, most people find "good health" a difficult goal to reach, how much more difficult it is for health workers to help others reach it. . . . It is this necessity for estimating the individual's need for momentary or hourly care, support, and encouragement, and health guidance that makes nursing a service of the highest order. Many of the activities involved are simple until their adjustments to the particular demands of the client or patient makes them complex. (Henderson, 1978, pp. 34-36)

Her insights into how her words might be misconstrued, however, did not prevent me from being critical of the implications of her words. Hindsight, I think I needed to take on mainstream nursing in order to forge my own way, but that was a period of tension in my dealings with Virginia, who had became a dear colleague.

But by the 1980s, I had changed my perspective once again, and I was viewing the definition differently. This was the decade when the American Nurses Association issued *Nursing. A Social Policy Statement* (1980), with its emphasis on nursing as dealing with individuals' responses to illness rather than with illness per se (the latter being the domain of medicine). This was an era when nurse practice acts sought to distinguish between the roles of physicians and nurses, so the latter would not be accused of practicing medicine without a license when they performed the same activities. Increasing attention was paid to the nursing diagnosis, as opposed to the medical diagnosis. Since this was a period when nurses with so-called expanded roles (e.g., as nurse practitioners) were too often described as "extenders of medical care," it seemed particularly important to identify the unique characteristics of nursing. As I watched these developments, I began to have renewed respect for Henderson's definition of nursing because it did not use the derivative language of medicine with its emphasis on diagnosis to describe nursing, and because it went well beyond focusing only on *patients' responses* to stipulating the overall goals of all nursing actions—health, recovery, and peaceful death. I looked upon Henderson's definition as an improvement over Nightingale's emphasis on putting the patient in the best condition for nature to act upon him, because hers was more all-inclusive. But I also regarded Henderson's definition as more substantial than an emphasis on *responses* to illness (actual or potential), because hers acknowledged the full range of patient outcomes.

Now that we are well into the 1990s, shaped by the move to managed care and self help, I have become even more admiring of Henderson's words. Her definition seems more timely now than ever before with its health orientation, implied commitment to hospice care ("peaceful death"), acknowledgment of the nurse as a "knowledge" worker, and support of consumer education. The buzz words of the day are quality, access, and cost effectiveness, and Henderson's definition implies those qualities and a general emphasis on primary care. Her definition speaks to many of the changes being currently advocated as if they were new—the shift away from "nurse at bedside" to the nurse being at the patient's side wherever that may be; the emphasis on the patient becoming independent of assistance as soon as possible.

Henderson always believed in a multidisciplinary approach to care with the various health care workers having overlapping functions. Though nursing is primarily care oriented and medicine is primarily cure oriented, Henderson understood that circumstances and settings regularly shape activities performed, and that they must continue to do so if the needs of the public are to be met. Indeed, she wondered in her writings if modifying nurse practice acts should be the focus, when a better solution might be to exempt professional nurses from the prohibition against the practice of medicine in specified situations. Henderson would also be comfortable with the current emphasis on outcomes research, because she so admired Florence Nightingale's work in demonstrating statistically the effects of nursing care on the recovery rate of soldiers in the military hospitals of the Crimea.

In this day and age when care is too often described in terms of a series of reimbursable services or productivity standards, Henderson offers most of all a general statement about nursing's purview that resonates possibly more today than it did when first written. Her professional nurse is a case manager committed to outcomes, but one who knows that discrete activities need to be embedded within overall health goals to which the patient subscribes, because it will be the patient who will bear the ultimate responsibility for achieving them once preliminary assistance has been provided. In this respect, Henderson is demonstrating that nursing's ethic is a feminist ethic. It is neither the simplistic admonition to "do good," nor the Judeo-Christian ethic "to do unto others as one would wish for oneself," with its disregard for possible cultural differences. Her ethic is customer minded, helping others do what they wish but do not yet know how to accomplish.

I could be accused of reading too much into Henderson's definition, but that is part of its enduring value—it continues to inspire those of us in the profession as a statement of our fundamental reason for being. Granted it focuses only on patients rather than families, communities, or health care delivery systems, but Henderson would be quick to agree that these larger units must be part of nursing's purview if one is to accomplish what she believes to be our core mandate. She never believed that the definition sufficed as all that needed to be said about nursing. The definition does, however, continue to serve us well in reminding us of what we are primarily about, and as such should enjoy renewed appreciation in these times when we seem too often rudderless.

I would argue that her definition isn't merely historically interesting but that it is futuristic in its emphasis and scope. In times of so much change, when job descriptions are constantly being revamped and systems are being reorganized, it has become commonplace to say that we are going in new directions where what we have done previously or what we have learned is likely not to be of much help. Such an approach can easily sow the seeds of antiintellectual thinking (the exact opposite of what Henderson was about), and leave all of us feeling discombobulated and paralyzed. It is in such times that we most need to hold onto that which is enduring. Henderson's definition offers us a wonderfully rich statement of who we are no matter what our organizational setting. It is our obligation to think through how her words can be best manifested in the next millennium.

References

American Nurses Association. (1980). *Nursing. A social policy statement.* Kansas City, Missouri: Author.

Henderson, V. (1978). Practice of and preparation for nursing. In V. Henderson & G. Nite (Eds.), *Principles and practice of nursing* (6th ed.) (pp. 3-121). New York: Macmillan.

McBride, A. B. (1976). *Living with contradictions: A married feminist.* New York: Harper & Row.

Virginia's Ashes

Kathleen T. Flynn, MS, RN
Chicopee, MA
Friend and Professional Colleague

"I *was fired from Teachers College* [Columbia University]," she said as she sewed additional button holes on a dress she had bought, was remaking, and planned to wear to the 1988 American Nurses Association convention where she would be honored. "Louise McManus [who was the director of the Nursing Education Division at Teachers College] wanted me to do committee work, but I thought clinical work was more important. I didn't mind leaving Teachers College. I was glad to do something else. I am telling you this for history to know."

This was a conversation where Miss Henderson talked and I listened, mostly without interruption. It was not all new to me. Over time I had observed that when she was interrupted with a question, she might change her focus. Not that the question interfered with her thought process, which was sharp and keen until age 95; maybe she didn't want to answer. But on this evening, her conversation was different; I had never heard about why she left Teachers College.

Her time at Teachers College (1934-1948) was not without conflict. There was conflict over her teaching. Director Isabel Stewart, who had preceded Mrs. McManus and resigned in 1947, "believed in the industrial model of organizing the way nursing care was delivered. Nurses were assigned to the tasks of patient care." Miss Henderson "believed in assigning a nurse to the patient with the nurse giving all the care to that patient." Miss Henderson was doing that with her students at Presbyterian Hospital in New York City where her long-time friends, nursing supervisors Cecile Covell and Marion Cleveland, and the Director of Nurses, Miss Helen Young, agreed with Miss Henderson (Flynn, 1997). Miss Stewart did not. Miss Henderson was called into Miss Stewart's office and was told that her teaching was unacceptable, and that what was important to her was the affection of her students. She was told that she wanted to be liked by her students. When the term *Primary Nursing* was coined in the 1970s, Miss Henderson said that is what she was doing in the 1940s, but she did not label it so. The nursing care plan was her idea too; she had searched the literature and nothing existed on the subject.

Committee work would take her away from nursing practice, she said, and thus there was no compromise. Miss Henderson left Teachers College. It was the end of being a faculty member in a school of nursing in a university. She never again had an official faculty position or a faculty title. Nor did she ever work in nursing service again or ever hold an elected office in a nursing organization. She worked alone the rest of her life as a private entrepreneur without the constraints of faculty or administrative work. She followed her own line of thinking about nursing and did what she thought was needed to be done, or what she thought should be done, or what others recognized as a need and asked her to do. She once said at a "flea market" party at her apartment on 164 Linden Street in New Haven that she hated to write and wrote because she was asked or encouraged to do so.

"It was for nursing." That was a reason and a theme I heard when in her later years she was awarded an honorary degree, or when a research day or library or something else was named in her honor. "It was for nursing." She represented the good in nursing in so many ways, both as a scholar and a gracious woman. She took a different road; it has made all the difference in the world. She was free, a luxury few can claim, and with that freedom came creativity, accountability, and work that has and will stand the test of time.

Leaving Teachers College was an end and a beginning. Out of the ashes of the firing came the twentieth century phoenix, the most celebrated nurse of the century with a national and international reputation who taught, influenced, and led generations of nurses who are and will be; who has received honors and recognition from national and international nursing organizations, colleges, and universities as she traveled the globe as nursing's good will ambassador; and who enjoyed nearly twenty-five years of celebration for her work when she was alive and well.

It is impossible for me to write about Miss Henderson or her influence on me and others without a discussion of her persona. She was a gracious lady, charming in her ways. She was a short woman (under 5 feet tall) with an uncoiffed hair style and characteristic style of dress; her social graces abounded and her charm, that one might attribute to Southern charm, is unforgettable. "It's mighty sweet of you to do that," was said frequently when she got a gift or a ride home from the grocery store, or when anyone did anything for her. She could be funny, direct, and disagree with a person's idea but not be disagreeable with the person. Professionally, she enjoyed the company of men, courted them with her charm, and could win a discussion like a CEO of a great corporation. She had the tenacity to achieve what she set out to achieve and her advice to me that evening as she sewed and talked of being fired was, "You've got to be tough inside. Inside." In those words, she described herself. She did like to be liked, like all of us. Her style of speech and timing of words captured her audience. She wrote letters, letters, and more letters. Sometimes I would mail ten or fifteen at a time. Her energy was not directed toward building a professional network in nursing, but she made contact with those in key positions or whose work she admired or was interested in, often for the purpose of giving, as she would say, "myaaaaa opinion." She was a remarkable woman whose company I enjoyed. She influenced me professionally, but personally her inner toughness, independence, strength, will, gracious charm, and courage were of equal importance. She had class!

In Greek and Egyptian mythology, the phoenix is a mythical bird reborn from its own ashes. Virginia's firing was the best thing that happened to her and for nursing. There is one phoenix at a time and it lives for hundreds of years. Virginia was almost 100 years old when she died in 1996—a twentieth century phoenix. Her work lives on.

Reference

Flynn, K.T. (1997). I remember Virginia A. Henderson. *Journal of Advanced Nursing, 25,* 648-651.

Influence

Virginia Dericks, MA, RN
Morristown, NJ;
Former student of Virginia Henderson at
Teachers College, Columbia University
New York, NY

It is not difficult to recall incidents and motivational forces in my professional life attributed to the influence of Virginia Henderson.

When I enrolled at Teachers College (TC), I was twenty-one years old and a recent graduate from a three-year hospital training school for nurses. As was prevalent in the 30s and 40s, the training hospital lacked a graduate nurse staff, so it was imperative to rely on student help to fulfill hospital needs. One learned by "experience."

Following graduation I felt the need for more education. I had no desire to teach; I simply wished more information to become a "regular nurse." My brother suggested a degree program, claiming, "A degree is useful, and you can receive better pay." In this frame of mind I enrolled at TC; and there began my long association with Virginia Henderson.

My first impression of Miss Henderson was of a small, friendly woman with a great deal of Southern charm. Despite a seemingly easygoing nature, I soon learned that high standards of performance were expected. As instructor, she had a professional presence. She was knowledgeable, experienced, and had written the textbook *Principles and Practice of Nursing*, considered to be the "bible" in nursing.

The central focus of Virginia's teaching was always the patient. Early on, she gave her definition of nursing, which was essentially, "Help patient to perform the daily activities contributing to health that he cannot perform by himself, such as bathing, recreation, etc; and teach the patient (and family) health practices they need to know." (*Activities of daily living [ADLs]* was not standardized in the nomenclature at that time.) Although a simple definition, hers was enlightening, for previously I had thought of nursing as a series of dutiful tasks, involving procedures, medications, doctors' orders, hospital regulations, and general body care. I was particularly impressed by Virginia's stand that patients' needs took precedence over strict adherence to hospital rules, such as unyielding visiting hours, bath and bedpan schedules, and doctors' orders without question.

Virginia used a great variety of teaching methods: group discussion, field trips, student projects, etc. She sought out living examples of persons currently engaged in clinical practice. I recall visiting the Neurological Institute where a nursing supervisor demonstrated the specialized care given to unconscious patients.

Virginia seemed equally respectful of professionals outside of nursing, utilizing their expertise to enhance concepts of total care. A hospital chaplain spoke to us on family grief and mourning; a physician explained a popular theory about body types and their relation to disease; and a cosmetologist talked about nail care. What impressed me was the natural ease with which Virginia discussed issues with these people.

The presentation of student projects was always a highlight for which Virginia strictly required the use of principles and documentation. For example, skin care needed to include the physiology of sweat glands, and urological drainage required the mention of studies in physics. I once participated in a three-student project to study oxygen concentrations in an oxygen tent. Although I had nursed pneumonia patients in tents, I was aghast when Virginia proposed we prove the oxygen concentrations in an actual tent with the flaps closed and open. We worked hard and long on the project, arranging for the loan of a tent and tank from a local oxygen supply company. Such approaches to care taught me to think, analyze, stretch my imagination, and value my own judgment.

Another time I presented a project to demonstrate the variety of literature available for teaching health practices. I traveled all over New York City (health department, schools, subways, hospitals, etc.) gathering materials. With three bulletin boards full of information, categorized according to health problem, plus sources where obtained, I received an A+. This was a major event for me, because I then began to see myself as "teacher."

Virginia also arranged for field experiences at nearby hospitals, making rounds to follow student progress. My "assignment" was a seriously ill man with pemphigus whose body was covered with blisters and bullae. They were so painful, he could not tolerate any clothes touching his skin. I recall devising a tent-like structure over his wheelchair to facilitate transportation to bath and treatment rooms.

For practice teaching, I taught a course in Home Nursing to professors' wives. I remember Virginia sitting at the back of the room critiquing the smallest details, such as posture, delivery, and voice. Among my souvenirs, I still have Virginia's detailed evaluation of my teaching.

Virginia was aware of us as people, too, inviting students to her apartment to celebrate a holiday or final exam with a home-cooked meal. Serious discussions inevitably followed. One time she asked, "Why do you keep referring to our gender as 'ladies'? What is wrong in calling us 'women'?" This was many years before the feminist movement!

Upon accepting my first teaching position, Virginia gave me a little book entitled *Talks to Teachers on Psychology*. It contained thoughts of the great educational philosophers, Dewey and Kilpatric. That book, as well as Harmer and Henderson, proved valuable to me for a long time.

During World War II, I had a conflict between joining the army and continuing to teach. So I visited Virginia to discuss this. Her thinking led me to believe I could do as much, or more, by remaining at home and teaching students in the Nurse Cadet Corps, which I did. Nowadays this process would be called *mentoring*. Then I simply regarded it as a continued friendly interest by someone wiser.

Virginia always maintained an interest in her former students and was delighted to hear what they were doing. I once invited her to my home to meet my family. While riding through the country, we stopped at a showcase barn to observe farmers milking prize cows. We found them using the "case method of assignment," with the farmers responsible for the same cow each day. It was explained that a cow gives more milk if a bond is created between the cow and farmer, and if milking is by hand rather than by machine. This greatly impressed Virginia, and the farmer asked her if she would like to try her hand. While milking the cow, I took her picture and still have it.

Following my MA degree in 1947, I spent the major part of my career at the Cornell University-New York Hospital School of Nursing and Medical Center. My first position carried a dual responsibility for both patient care and teaching. This provided an excellent opportunity for remaining "patient centered," and for coordinating class instruction with clinical assignments. My varied teaching methods certainly had their origins in classes taught by Virginia.

During this period I wrote the chapter on *Postoperative Care* for Harmer and Henderson. I recall Virginia critiquing it and my having to rewrite it in order to include additional sources. To illustrate the text, Virginia asked former students to pose for photos. In an early edition there is a photo of "Nurse instructing a patient in colostomy irrigation," with Virginia as patient and myself as nurse.

After an interval in Public Health Nursing, I returned to the CU-NYH Medical Center in 1966 to develop the role of Clinical Nurse Specialist (CNS) around the care of ostomy patients. By this time, Virginia's philosophy had been well integrated into my thinking and was part of me. Obviously, ostomy care concerned a person's inability to control an important daily function, elimination. And the consequences of unpredictable drainage affected all ADLs, including sleep, mobilization, etc.

My development of self as "expert" centered in direct patient care. Teaching, consultation, and empirical research followed closely as natural outgrowths. The CNS role evolved progressively, derived from a culmination of varied nursing experiences, from the early years with Virginia Henderson to my retirement in 1984.

In conclusion, Virginia Henderson was one of the most learned persons I ever knew, with capability of channeling her knowledge into nursing practice, no matter what the setting. Her attributes as a caring teacher and mentor contributed immensely to my long and satisfying professional career.

A great woman!

Peanut Coaches Miss Foley

Mary T. Foley Carew, MA, RN
Venice, FL;
Former Student of Virginia Henderson at
Teachers College, Columbia University
New York, NY

When I was invited to share in the festschrift to honor Virginia Henderson, I immediately replied that she had been a great influence on my life, professionally. However, please understand that many years have gone by and so my memories are somewhat hazy.

I received my RN over fifty years ago, and shortly thereafter received my BS and MA degrees from Teachers College, Columbia University. Professionally, I was engaged in the teaching of medical-surgical nursing in hospital schools, public health nursing, and in health education as a school nurse-teacher in several schools.

Virginia Henderson was one of my professors at Teachers College, in the teaching of nursing education. Since this was my major, I had a number of classes with her, some on a one-to-one basis, some in small classes, some in actual field work. She was tiny in stature and referred to as "Peanut." She was highly respected, and it was easy to set up a rapport with her.

My practice teaching was during World War II. The subject was Home Nursing sponsored by the American Red Cross. My students were members of the faculty at Teachers College. (Incidentally, as I remember, Virginia Henderson volunteered to teach a similar course.) Before and after each lesson, we would sit in her office and she would critique my lesson plan: the content based on scientific data, the outline to be put on the blackboard, the objectives of each lesson considered, a bulletin board display planned, even a flower arrangement procured for a patient's bedside tray, etc. In her critique she might say, "Miss Foley, your voice is too nasal; your posture could be improved; you stand with your abdomen thrust forward; when talking to your class try to capture the students attention by focusing on one student at a time by making eye to eye contact." She was like a director or coach of a dramatic play. If I answered a question casually or superficially, she would tell me so. I remember her saying to me, "Miss Foley, I know you can do better."

Consequently, I learned to become very knowledgeable about my subjects, and I felt confident about my teaching. All this preparation proved invaluable to me in my professional experiences. In all my classes, the outline was on the blackboard, the objectives of each lesson considered, quizzes were prepared, etc. On several occasions, I was observed by my school principal for evaluation; fortunately, I could always use the techniques that I had learned in Virginia Henderson's class.

In the small classes that Professor Henderson gave, she would provoke class discussions by asking questions on the emerging current problems and debatable issues in the field of nursing. There were many changes occurring in nursing practice. Nurses were assuming more responsibilities; they were not so docile in their relationships with doctors. They were becoming partners in patient care with the medical profession. Virginia Henderson recognized these changes, and she was in the forefront of addressing them. Remember, this was in the early 40s; hospital schools of nursing were just diminishing, and the BS degrees were just replacing them. The war was on; integration was taking place. These made for interesting class discussions. Virginia Henderson often invited members of her class to her house for afternoon tea, coffee, hot chocolate with whipped cream, and desserts. The conversation was directed to current problems; we were way ahead of "women's lib"—by far.

Another course she taught was related to the clinical care of patients. This course involved field experiences. One program was at a New York hospital. In this course, Virginia Henderson stressed the care of the patient by promoting patient care plans. Students were assigned several patients for their bedside care. Before giving care, we would make a plan considering their personal needs such as his or her preferences about hygienic care, fluid intake, elimination, foot care, arranging for treatments, etc. I can remember taking care of several patients; one in particular required oral mouth care after major oral surgery. She was objecting to the procedure even though it was effective, so I then requested a change of assignment. Round table discussions followed these assignments of patient care. We would present our patient, with his or her medical condition, problems encountered in hospital care, social problems, plans for home care, etc. Miss Henderson complimented me for recognizing the above problem. I liked the patient care plans. They helped organize your assignment. The patient knew when he or she would receive care and what to expect. You could learn to understand your patient. I also used them when I was teaching surgical nursing in the clinical area, as well as patient case studies. Just to digress for a moment, in 1990, my husband had a major stroke and required constant nursing care until his death in 1993. For his care, I arranged to have several health aides assist me. We followed a plan similar to Professor Henderson's course. Can you imagine, some fifty years later finding how useful and effective these plans were. Two of the aides went on to become LPNs. They have personally thanked me for the guidance they received.

I also remember that when I was studying for my master's dissertation, Virginia Henderson would emphasize to me that it was important to "master" the subject, so that it would prove meaningful to me. My mother was dying at that time, so it was a very difficult time for me, but Virginia Henderson was very considerate and allowed me an extension of several reports that were due.

I am very grateful to Virginia Henderson for inspiring me to become a "professional" RN. She was my advisor. I could relate to her, and I was able to incorporate these feelings into my personal and professional life. Incidentally, my daughter Mary, who has her BS degree in nursing, pointed out to me that Virginia Henderson was way ahead of her time; she said that we were in the forefront for changes in nursing. My daughter-in-law, Molly, has her BS in nursing. She is now studying to become a Family Nurse Practitioner at a university college of nursing. As a matter of fact, only last year, she called me and asked me if I knew Virginia Henderson. It seems that she was taking a course on Theories of Nursing and they cited Virginia Henderson as one of the outstanding theorists in the field of nursing; coincidentally, my granddaughter, Maura, discovered my copy of Virginia Henderson's book (4th edition) in their book shelf. It is autographed with the following inscription to me: "Mary T. Foley—With admiration and affection. Virginia Henderson. 1942." I treasure this.

Part III
Humanitarianism

We're Two Peas in a Pod

Charles H. Burdge, Jr., MFA
Killingworth, CT
Great nephew of Virginia Henderson

O***ur 5-year-old daughter***, Lucy, is one of Virginia's great-great nieces. Lucy was born early in the evening on December 26, 1991. Virginia said, "When word of Lucy's birth reached us at Bellevue, my poor, old, gray head went pink."

Their first meeting came a few weeks later. The colicky Lucy studied Virginia's countenance and fell peacefully to sleep in her arms. "We're two peas in a pod," Virginia whispered to the sleeping baby.

Several months later, Lucy fell asleep moments before her christening ceremony. As the sacrament was administered, Lucy awoke crying. Ever supportive, Virginia's voice rose above and cut through the din, "I'd be bawlin' too, if someone poured water on my head while I was napping." The laughter and Virginia's voice soothed and quieted the startled Lucy.

Whether at Bellevue, Linden Street, our house, or wherever it was they "cozied-up," Virginia and Lucy couldn't seem to get enough of each other.

Lucy was there waiting the day when Virginia arrived to make her acquaintance with her new apartment and her new life in Guilford. Lucy had been asking questions; she had overheard conversations, and she knew Virginia had left Bellevue for the last time. She was now nearly $2^1/_2$ years old, and in big girl fashion, insisted on wearing her best dress and shoes to welcome and cheer up her pal.

A basket overflowing with stuffed toy animals was placed in the living room beside a child's chair. Lucy introduced Virginia to the toy animals by tickling her with each one and growling. Virginia sat on her sofa feigning terror, as assorted officials explained the rules of her new establishment.

During this time, Lucy wore a dress twice a week—to go to church and to go to Virginia's. She appeared from Virginia's bedroom one day with chocolate smudges all over her face, fingers and dress. "Did you find my bedside kisses?" Virginia asked through her giggles. "No!" came Lucy's indignant reply. Virginia howled with laughter, then quickly asked that Lucy not be scolded. "I want her to be happy here."

Virginia's sofa became Lucy's trampoline, the walker served as monkey bars, and the living room carpet was a gym mat.

Lucy was about to start nursery school two mornings a week in September that year. She told Virginia that she was afraid she might cry when left on her own for the first time at school. Virginia had her sit beside her on the sofa. She patted Lucy's hand while gathering her thoughts. "Crying is a proper thing, a good thing," she said. She then pointed to the large portrait that hung on the wall behind them. "That's my mother. Her name was Lucy. When I'm lonely and scared, I remember her best. You won't be alone. Don't be scared. Go on and cry— but not for too long—then go find some fun."

At the next week's visit, Virginia asked Lucy how she liked school. Lucy told Virginia that her classmate, Andrew, had bitten her. Virginia was horrified, "Why did he bite you, honey?" "Because I roughed him up," said Lucy meekly. Then looking straight into Virginia's twinkling eyes, Lucy proclaimed, "I can handle the bullies at school."

As Virginia grew weaker, Lucy used her "outdoor voice" when speaking to her. She especially enjoyed shouting her newest knock-knock jokes while pushing Virginia in her wheelchair down the long echoing hallways.

Lucy would stand proudly reciting her alphabet and numbers before Virginia. And sit cuddling with her on the sofa explaining drawings she'd done in school for Virginia.

Lucy was a little over 4 years old when Virginia died. She'd gone to Hospice to say good-bye a few days before.

When word came the morning of her death, Lucy softly said, "Oh, that's too bad." Later in the day, Lucy was riding quietly on the back seat of the car. "Virginia's up in heaven, isn't she?" she asked. I said, "Yes. She's laughing and having a good time the way she always did when we'd visit." Lucy pounded the back seat with her fist and shouted angrily, "No she's not!" "Lucy, you don't think Virginia is happy?" I asked. "No, because I'm not with her!"

Virginia, My Aunt . . . and Mother

Delia H. Mark, BA, BS, RN
School Nurse
Stuart Country Day School
Princeton, NJ
Niece of Virginia Henderson

As ***a child*** growing up in Richmond, Virginia, one of my happiest memories is that of my aunt, Virginia Henderson. She was living in New York, which to me at that age was in another world. I knew as young as seven or eight that I wanted to be a nurse because Virginia was. I spent summers in Appomattox, Virginia with my mother's family, and every Sunday my parents and I would go to "Trivium," the family home in Bedford County. Virginia was always there to greet us, and there was an air of excitement when she appeared. She was ready to have fun and to show her love for everyone. Of course, there was always something special for me on those occasions. One I particularly remember is having a doll tea party in the garden with a real china tea set!

My mother died when I was thirteen, and it was decided that I would live with my father's family at Trivium, as he traveled quite a bit. My grandmother and my aunts, Jane, Lucy, Frances, and Virginia, and my uncle Louis Houff, became my immediate family. It was really Virginia who was "in charge of me." It was decided that I would go to boarding school. Virginia came down for the summer with a new wardrobe for me, and the entire summer was spent in preparation. Name tags, stationery, etc. had to be purchased, and Virginia did all of this. She opened a checking account for me and essentially taught me how to take care of myself. Virginia not only paid my boarding school tuition, but college and nursing school.

Virginia was always there on special occasions. She called me regularly to see how I was. Many times when I went to get my allowance (which Virginia had sent) from the headmistress, she would tell me that Virginia had called to see how I was.

I remember being at Trivium for summer vacation and preparing for Virginia's visits. She was a nurse so everything had to be "spanking" clean. I used to tease the family later, saying they didn't make such a to-do about my visits as they did Virginia's! The time Virginia spent with us was like magic. There was always something exciting going on. No one was ever bored when Virginia was at home! She loved her family dearly and would do anything for them.

College time came for me, and Virginia was in charge of helping me select a college. She was there for my graduation and "hooded" me, as they said. My dream about nursing school was coming true. It was decided that I would go to Columbia Presbyterian School of Nursing. Virginia's apartment on Morningside Drive in New York became a haven for me and my friends. The door was always open for meals or just to chat. To this day my friends still look upon Virginia as their family too.

I graduated from nursing school and three years later married a man whom Virginia looked upon as a son. Virginia bought his "trousseau" and made most of mine, including altering my aunt's wedding dress. She, my other aunts, and my uncle gave us a beautiful wedding.

Then came our daughter Catherine, who was the apple of her eye. The minute I went to the hospital Virginia was on the train to Boston to be there to help us. Her proudest moment was when Catherine graduated from the Yale School of Nursing. When Catherine married Charles Burdge, Virginia was most happy, as Charlie was one of her favorite people. I mention Catherine and Charlie because when Virginia was at The Gables and then at Hospice, they were the family members who were in charge of her care. Charlie visited her often with the children of whom Virginia was so proud.

I have remembered many important events in my life to show what an influence Virginia had on our immediate family's lives. Reverend Bliss said at the memorial service held for Virginia at Battell Chapel, Yale University, last year that Virginia once said that she always wanted to be an architect and a mother. She was both, and as he and her grave stone say, "an architect of nursing and a mother to all of us" . . . especially to me.

From Papers to Person

Susan M. Reverby, PhD
Professor of Women's Studies
Wellesley College
Wellesley, MA

A ***student once asked me*** what the difference was between history and anthropology. Breathing a slight sigh of relief, I somewhat flippantly told her, "The historian's informants are dead." But as I got pulled (somewhat kicking and screaming) into doing twentieth century history, this differentiation did not hold. Twentieth century "informants" often leave to an archive their correspondence, personal musings, copies of their publications—and stay alive at the same time. The historian who works on their lives then has a dilemma: she develops a sense of who the person is and what they have done, usually first from their papers and from what others have said about them. But she may also have the chance to actually meet them. There is, however, something peculiar about interviewing someone whose thoughts and actions from fifty years earlier you have already absorbed. Who is the "real" person: your historical creation or the human being who stands in front of you? Do you have to choose?

I first met Virginia Henderson on "paper" when I was a graduate student in American Studies at Boston University (BU) in the 1970s. I had already written some about nursing in an earlier career as a health policy analyst (but nonnurse) and had fallen in historical love with many of nursing's early twentieth century leaders: Lavinia Dock, M. Adelaide Nutting, Lillian Wald. Henderson was a name I did not yet know as I made my way out of the ninteenth century for my dissertation in volume after volume of the various nursing and hospital journals.

Because of my topic, my wise History Department thesis advisor sent me off to BU's still extant nursing school to find Mary Ann Garrigan, the founder of the Nursing Archives in the university's Mugar Library. Miss Garrigan, I was assured, would make sure I was getting the right sources.

"You've used the Henderson index, of course," the rather formidable Miss Garrigan thundered at me after I passed what seemed like the first of her nursing "begats" test by at least knowing that Isabel Stewart came *after* Linda Richards and Isabel Hampton Robb."

"No," I replied honestly, "I have not."

"Well," Miss Garrigan immediately retorted, "you cannot write about nursing's history in the twentieth century if you don't work with what Virginia Henderson has done."

Mary Ann Garrigan was certainly right. I walked the three long blocks back to Mugar Library and found the four volumes of painstaking labor of love: a guide to all of the nursing literature up until the late 1950s, carefully indexed and cross-indexed. I couldn't believe that someone had actually done all of this, how much it meant for my work and for countless other historians of nursing and American health care.

In addition, it turned out that Miss Henderson had also given her papers to the Nursing Archives. The finding aid/index to her papers barely prepared me for what I was going to find. Spilling out of the boxes and acid-free papers came a person: vibrantly devoted to nursing, a theorist trying to make sense of what it meant to actually care for patients, a loving friend to nurses everywhere in the world, a Southerner with charm, passion and deep concern for every kind of human being. There were also letters between Henderson and Annie Goodrich of Yale, reflecting decades of letter writing and slow role reversals as they both aged. There were painful reports that hinted at the struggles at Teachers College. It was a trove of materials, most of which I went through but could not yet see how to use in the work I was then doing.

Several years later, after I had finished my dissertation and book, I came back to Virginia Henderson (Reverby, 1987). I had begun to teach Women's Studies at Wellesley College in the early 1980s, and the debates were then raging over whether or not women did science differently than men. Much of the argument took place in the rather heady theory areas of philosophy and history of science. At one scholarly meeting on the topic, I remember asking a leading philosopher, "But how did actual women use these differing conceptions of science in their work?" When I realized she could not answer my question, I went back to Virginia Henderson for my own search.

This search took me back to BU, but also to the papers of the Department of Nursing and Health at Columbia University's Teachers College (TC) where Henderson had spent much of the 1930s and 1940s. It was in these papers at the TC Archives that I "re-met" Henderson. This time I found a woman who loved science, who had been educated at TC by Martha Ruth Smith, a nurse trying desperately to have laboratory testing and scientific methods ". . . serve the art of nursing" (Smith, 1932, p. 182). Henderson took to her teachings. How was she going to make scientific methods and clinical practice come together? How could the art and science of nursing meld?

I spent days in the archives, reading through report after report as Henderson tried to make others see what she saw in the 1930s and 1940s: that nursing's professional growth had to come by using science in clinical practice, not merely as a method, but as theory and practice (Baer, 1987; Reverby, 1989). As I read I had a picture of Henderson that formed in my head: as a fighter and as a theorist with a passion for the work of nurses in their daily lives.

Then I realized, or was told, that she was still very much alive, and very much willing to be interviewed. It was thus with both trepidation and my rather bulging pregnant body that I took the train from Boston to New Haven to meet with Miss Henderson. Although I had seen pictures of her, somehow she was in my mind a giant in the field (and at 5′3″ myself, everyone else has always been taller). What I hadn't expected was someone shorter than me but with a warmth and caring that was immediate at the greeting and demonstrated, once again, that a spirit increases one's presence and size.

I was taken into the living room, served tea in beautiful cups, and felt as if I were whisked back into another time period. I don't think I will ever forget the oriental rug in the bathroom and the elegance of the apartment. But there was nothing reticent, stuffy, or old-fashioned about this woman. She seemed somewhat amazed I had read as much about her as I had. At times it did seem awkward. Could I really ask about the demands Annie Goodrich made on her in her last days? Could I really ask her about what happened those last years at Teachers College? Had I gotten her views on science and the struggle to implement them right?

Yet she seemed more than willing to speak her truths. She giggled and talked about aging, and how it made it possible for you to say what was on your mind. We talked honestly about the difficulties and dilemmas that nursing faced from the 1920s to the present. She was careful when she was critical of others, but she also had the sense that history had indeed vindicated her views and rewarded her patience. As I was leaving, she inquired about my pregnancy, told me to take Vitamin C for my impending cold, and gave me a small gift to give to my eight-year-old at home.

I got to see Virginia Henderson a number of other times. I was delighted to speak at her ninetieth birthday celebration a few years later at Yale. I participated in a "Conversations with Virginia Henderson" for the Lowell-Fitchburg, Massachusetts nursing programs. She read and critiqued the article I wrote about her. The "paper" Virginia Henderson and the "person" melded in my mind and in my writing. And I was very honored, humbled, and glad that my "informant" had lived along with her papers—as vibrant, honest, and thoughtful a woman as I ever hope to be.

References

Baer, E. (1987). 'A cooperative venture' in pursuit of professional status: A research journal for nursing. *Nursing Research, 35*, 18-35.

Reverby, S. (1987). *Ordered to care: The dilemma of American nursing*. New York: Cambridge University Press.

Reverby, S. (1989). A legitimate relationship: Nursing, hospitals and science in the twentieth century. In D. Long, & J. Golden (Eds.), *The American general hospital: Communities and social contexts* (pp. 135-156). Ithaca: Cornell University Press.

Smith, M. (1932). The improvement of nursing methods. *38th Annual Report of the National League of Nursing Education*, New York: National League of Nursing Education.

Gifts

Ruth N. Knollmueller, PhD, RN
Associate Director of Nursing
University of Kentucky College of Nursing
University of Kentucky Center for Rural Health
Hazard, KY

Each relationship that one has with another person has unique qualities that make it a special one. One of the basic elements in any relationship is that it is mutual. That, in itself, is a gift and begins to define friendships. The unique aspects of the more than thirty years that I had known Virginia Henderson can be described in the acronym *GIFTS* (*G*ifts, *I*con, *F*riend, *T*eacher, *S*age).

Gifts: Whenever she could, Virginia would give a gift. If it was a hostess gift, she often placed assorted items into a shopping bag for the host (and in my case, including our two daughters) to select any article of choice. Other times she would make the selection herself. Her gifts included things she had purchased. It was also a lovely way for her to share with others articles that she had received on her many travels. For example, Virginia had been given a rectangular tapestry (12″ × 18″), in a black, brown, burnt orange, and gold pattern fringed on the long ends, from the Director of Nursing at the Aga Khan University Medical Center in Pakistan when she had been invited to speak at the opening of the new hospital facility there in the early 1980s. She gave this tapestry to me in 1984 on one of her visits to dinner at our home.

One Saturday in the spring of 1962 when I was living in New Haven, Connecticut, my roommate, Barbara Anderson (Johnson) and I took a train into New York City to see the Broadway musical play, *Carousel.* Upon arriving home very late that night, we were met at the train station by three friends who informed us that there had been a fire and all of our clothes were destroyed. When Barbara arrived for her classes at the Yale University School of Nursing where she was a student, on Tuesday following the fire there was a package for her with a card signed, "From a friend." It was a new outfit from Ann Taylor. Twenty-five years later, Virginia told me she had stopped on her way home from work having heard about the fire and made that purchase and arranged for it to be delivered anonymously to the School of Nursing.

Icon: In August 1983 I was invited to speak at the Katholische Akademie School of Nursing in Regensburg, Germany. Just outside the lecture hall was a bulletin board on the long wall facing the corridor. It had a photo and text display of three nursing leaders: Florence Nightingale, Agnes Karll, and Virginia Henderson. When I began speaking to the roomful of students, I started by commenting on that lovely display and explained that I knew Virginia Henderson as my friend. The students audibly gasped or clasped their hands and reverently replied (for it was a Catholic postgraduate school) and asked in awesome voices, "You are a friend of Miss Henderson?" Later I sent this school a copy of the book, *Principles and Practice of Nursing* (Henderson and Nite, 1978), which Virginia autographed. I visited the school a few years later and observed this book in a lighted glass case in the library.

Friend: Virginia knew who her friends were and whom she could call and ask for a favor. Usually it was for a ride or for some simple personal need. She had numerous friends whom she could contact so that she did not wear any one person out. She was generous with her friendships, especially with students. Former students would write to her, and she kept a lively correspondence going with many of them and with many other people. She received each person as an individual and corresponded with them accordingly. Hostess notes thanking for an invitation were a way of life for her, and those of us who received them now treasure them. Frequently when I visited her, she would hand me a fistful of letters she had written asking that I mail them for her.

In 1972 she required a photograph to use for her various speaking engagements and asked me to do it. As a result, the picture she used for professional purposes for the next twenty years or so was one she asked me to take of her in her office at the Yale University School of Nursing. Her favorite was one taken with a photograph of Annie W. Goodrich in the background. Actually, she liked the background and selected another photograph I took of her that she liked better and superimposed it on that one of her with Goodrich and used that as her choice for use for reproduction purposes. The last time that this photograph was used was for the announcement of her death in the *New York Times.* A memorable benedictory for me.

Our last time together occurred on New Year's Eve Day 1995 when I, along with three other dear friends, spent the afternoon with her. Virginia was responsive when a Christmas cactus was presented to her and while we socialized around her dining area table that looked out onto a beautiful expanse of nature with trees, birds, and lovely grounds. It reminded me of the time in 1985 when there was a fire in the stairwell of her Linden Street apartment in New Haven, Connecticut between Christmas and New Year's, requiring her to relocate for a time. She was moved into temporary quarters a couple of blocks away. A colleague and I on our way to visiting her stopped at a grocery store to pick up a few of what we knew were her favorite food items (yes, ice cream was one item) and knocked on her door. She opened it and exclaimed, "Oh, wonderful, my two favorite public health nurses . . ."

In 1986 Virginia was on her way to a speaking engagement in Spain when the limousine from New Haven to Kennedy Airport in New York hydroplaned in Jamaica, New York and she hit the back of her head, causing a six-inch laceration. After a brief hospitalization for observation and sutures to the laceration, Virginia returned to her apartment but could not rest well because of pain, stiffness, and general soreness to her body. A couple of us helped her unpack her suitcase for Spain and repack it for another brief hospitalization locally where she could recover for a few days from severe sleep deprivation and bruises. Recover she did.

TEACHER: Virginia was the Grande Dame of teaching. She might be occupying the chair, a stool, or a place on a couch where she was often surrounded by learners of all ages. Always in the circle of people there was active and animated discussion. Her knowledge was eclectic and vast. She had lived through so many years of nursing. I recall being a part of informal social sessions in the early 1970s where Virginia talked about the early leaders in nursing, especially the work and life of Annie W. Goodrich.

During her prime years of teaching she focused on clinical nursing, which may have resulted in her being invited to write a fundamentals textbook for beginning nurses that had originally been done by Bertha Harmer. Later she was an avid supporter of the use of library resources and often did classes for students on that topic.

Her textbook, *Principles and Practice of Nursing*, was a tome of information. On page 432 of that 1978 volume is Figure 5-27, labeled "A normal female karyotype . . .," which is the report of a chromosome study of my first daughter. This adds a unique personal dimension for me in this text.

Travel for Virginia really began in earnest after she was sixty years old when she was frequently invited to speak and to teach from the podium. Her forum included the United States and many foreign countries.

When spending her last weeks of life at The Connecticut Hospice in Branford, Connecticut, Virginia continued to teach, this time by her presence and through her past writings. Nurses who knew Virginia because they had learned her definition of nursing when in school informed other nurses who also cared for her but did not know either Virginia or her writings.

SAGE: Virginia thrived on discussing issues with young people and seemed to be sought out by them for ideas and opinions. She always loved to give her opinion—one of the blessings of her age, she'd say. She enjoyed telling memories of her associations with Annie W. Goodrich, founding dean of the Yale University School of Nursing; Lillian Wald and Lavinia Dock, founders of the Henry Street Visiting Nurse Service; Marion Sheahan, public health nursing leader in New York state and later in the federal system; and others who were leaders when Virginia was coming along in the profession of nursing. She was nurtured by sages of her era and became a mentor to many others over the years.

Beyond the material gifts that Virginia gave to friends, colleagues, or visitors was the generosity of her time and counsel to a host of people. To some she was an icon; to me she was a friend, teacher, and sage.

Reference

Henderson, V., & Nite, G. (1978). *Principles and Practice of Nursing* (6th ed.). New York: Macmillan, 432.

Memories

Lucie S. Kelly, PhD, RN, FAAN
Professor Emeritus
Columbia University School of Public Health & Nursing
New York, NY
President (1983-85) Sigma Theta Tau

H***ow could one not think warmly*** of Virginia Henderson? Modern, even avant–garde in her professional thinking, there was something old-fashioned and ladylike in her human relations—something that, sadly, seems to be lost or nearly lost as we hurry to our future. Not only has Virginia had a lasting impact on my professional life, but she remains tucked in a small part of my heart for her humanness.

I simply can't remember the authors of any of the textbooks used as a basic baccalaureate student except one—Harmer and Henderson. (After all, it has been fifty years, but in all honesty, I probably didn't remember them five years later.) But Harmer and Henderson was a nursing bible. Before I dreamed of writing nursing textbooks myself, I was in awe of the vast amount of knowledge and common sense in that book and wondered about the authors. Perhaps that was even the beginning of an inspirational twinge about writing a book for future students.

However, that was long before I met that mythical figure—Virginia Henderson. I can't remember that first meeting as to where or when, except that then and later, she was always warm and interested in whatever the topic. Once, in Jerusalem at a Sigma Theta Tau research meeting, we had a long leisurely dinner together and talked about personal and professional things. I always felt that I was having contact with a historical figure, even though we met rather frequently at professional meetings.

Whether Virginia ever thought of herself that way, I'll never know, but I cherish the handwritten notes she wrote to me, usually after she had read something I'd written, including my books. This wasn't just a courteous gesture; her comments indicated that she had read and thought about certain aspects. I especially enjoyed one where she commended my common-sense approach to a rather esoteric subject about which we in nursing tend to get ourselves in an uproar!

Being a history buff, I can't help being grateful that I, and I'm sure a number of others, were recipients of her personal letters. When I research the lives of our early nursing leaders, I am always impressed that the most "real" impression of these fantastic women comes not from their accomplishments, outstanding though they might be, but rather from the correspondence from, to, and about them. E-mail and telephone calls have replaced much of the professional and personal correspondence we have today. Will our knowledge of the thoughts, the personality, and even the style of our living nursing leaders be missing for some future generation? Of course, we have their published writings and often, fortunately their images on videotape. And depending on the situation, that does give us something not available in the late nineteenth and early twentieth century, even though these are on-stage events. But what about those little personal glimpses caught in a brief informal note? Ah, Virginia, I'm so glad I have those tangible remembrances of you! They meant a lot to me when I received them, and now I touch history when I read them again.

A Life of Love and Service

Meghan M. Fitzgerald, BA
Longmeadow, MA
Class of 1997, University of Notre Dame

I *was a hostess* at a private party celebrating the ninetieth birthday of "The Most Famous Nurse in the World," an event and a meeting forever etched in my mind. I was twelve years old at the time, and entering Miss Henderson's home on Linden Street in New Haven that day was like entering the world. Nurses, academics, admirers, and friends had traveled from foreign reaches such as France, Japan, and the United Kingdom to celebrate with Miss Virginia Henderson. In the air was the delicious aroma of sweetmeats, sandwiches, fresh fruit, and chocolates prepared for the guests. As Miss Henderson supervised the finishing touches on those Epicurean delights, she graciously welcomed me to her home. When I took on the role of server, I found it hard to believe that it was *her* day, for she was not staged in the limelight but played a modest role working along side those in the kitchen and mingling with her guests.

Six years later, I began to research her life for a biography that I was writing for my Senior Advanced Placement English class in high school. It was then that I realized I should not have been surprised that Miss Henderson behaved as she did on her ninetieth birthday. Her mild manner and hands-on approach to her celebration in 1987 mirrored her lifelong personal and hands-on devotion to nursing and patient care.

The process of corresponding with her family, friends, colleagues, and former students during my research process served as a testament to Miss Henderson. Every person to whom I wrote or sought to interview enthusiastically answered my call. As I was assimilating their stories of her life, I became infected by Miss Henderson. In the same way that she had put her whole self into nursing, I found myself wanting to put all my strength into discovering her. I began to find that just like literature, the lives of people have themes, too. Miss Henderson's emerged naturally. Her work and her life exhibited the words of Kahlil Gibran in *The Prophet*, "Work is love made visible." From there I entitled my paper, *Virginia Avenel Henderson: A Life of Love and Service.*

Before I completed the biography, my aunt, Kathleen Flynn, a nurse and colleague of Miss Henderson, took me to visit Miss Henderson again. That was in March of 1993 when

I was eighteen years old. At that time Miss Henderson was living at her new residence, called "The Gables," in Guilford, Connecticut, a place that offered her "assisted living." There she had a one-bedroom apartment with a housekeeping service and a nurse who checked on her regularly. She had the option of eating in her apartment or in a common dining room. As I looked around her apartment, admiring the fine pieces and collections I had seen at Linden Street, I was as charmed then as I had been when I first met her at her ninetieth birthday party.

More than ever before, I also had the impression that, in spite of her many contributions and honors, Miss Henderson was a humble woman. For two hours I sat before Miss Henderson in awe. Next to her on the couch were six books. The one that caught my eye was *Faces in Caring: The One Hundred Most Caring People in History* by Val Halamandaris. Curious to see if Miss Henderson was included in it, I asked her about it. Picking it up, she opened to the message her friend had written to her, proud to have had him sign it. I was not expecting her to show me his inscription, but rather the page of the book on which she was featured.

Being one of a hundred in the world is no small accomplishment. Yet, in order to see if Miss Henderson was one of the figures portrayed in the book, I had to ask to look at it myself. I passed by the entries of Jesus Christ, Thomas Jefferson, Gandhi, and Mother Teresa, knowing that the section on Virginia Henderson would be coming soon. I never felt so privileged to be in the presence of another person as I did that morning. I felt unworthy to be sitting one foot away from her, casually conversing. I wanted to dash out the door and tell the world all about this fascinating woman.

Although I would have loved to hear her talk about herself, she kept directing questions to me concerning my life, what I was going to do after high school, or making sure that I had something to eat because she "would feel like she was not a good hostess if her guests did not eat something."

My aunt could hardly tear me away from Miss Henderson. As we walked with her down to the dining room for lunch, we met the administrator of "The Gables." The administrator, who was giving a tour of the complex to the daughter of a prospective resident, introduced her to Miss Henderson as the former Dean of Yale School of Nursing. With an acuteness unmatched by any human being of her age, Miss Henderson indicated that she had never held that position. She mentioned that her work on the *Nursing Studies Index* would not have allowed her the time to be Dean. Trying to set the record straight, my aunt stated, "She's the most famous nurse in the world and her definition of nursing is most widely quoted." The client inquired about the definition. As if she had just written it for the fifth edition of the *Textbook of the Principles and Practice of Nursing*, Miss Henderson replied, "I say the nurse should do for the patient what he would do if he had the strength, the will, and the knowledge." Only tears, not words, can describe how I left Miss Henderson that day.

Her Uniqueness Was Her Strength

Melanie C. Dreher, PhD, RN, FAAN
Dean and Professor
University of Iowa College of Nursing
Iowa City, IA
President (1995-97) Sigma Theta Tau

A*s the current president* of Sigma Theta Tau International, I knew that I would be called upon to contribute to this festschrift for our esteemed Virginia Henderson, and frankly, I avoided it as long as possible. I'm not sure why. Certainly, it was not from a lack of things to say. Virginia Henderson's long career in nursing is teeming with interesting and laudable accomplishments. Her contributions to the development of the nursing profession in the United States and internationally could fill pages. But I wondered whether I could find the words that would even begin to capture adequately the spirit and essence of Virginia Henderson. Finally, I decided there were no words that could do that and instead I would simply tell the story of one magical evening in her company.

I believe it was the ANA meeting in Boston, perhaps 1992. I know that she already was in her nineties. The seemingly endless line of pant-suited delegates, eager to get on with the business of nursing governance, snaked from the registration desk through the lobby until it was nearly full. Since I had driven in from Amherst, I arrived before the crowd and was only fourth from the desk. As I turned to look at the crowd that had gathered behind me, I happened to see Virginia Henderson coming through the door, toting her small and ancient suitcase. She had taken the bus from New Haven. Smiling her inimitable smile, she joined the end of the line and, resting her bag on the floor, began to canvass the lobby. She was a good half hour from the registration counter.

I stepped forward and asked those at the front if they would mind allowing Virginia Henderson to go ahead of them and register. Of course, there was enthusiastic consent all around. I then went to Miss Henderson, picked up her bag, and the sea of nurses parted as Virginia Henderson walked unceremoniously but confidently, at once diminutive yet statuesque, smiling appreciatively but not obsequiously. As we stood at the registration counter, I decided that I was in for the long haul and, in spite of the fact that I had not yet registered myself, I knew I had no choice but to assure that her bag was carried to her room.

As we stood at the registration desk, which was about eye-level for Miss Henderson, I asked if she had plans for the evening and was surprised to learn that she had none. It was just like her to live in the present, without future plans, and enjoy every moment of it.

We made arrangements to go to dinner. I was thrilled at the prospect of spending the evening in the company of this extraordinary person, this woman, this nurse whom I admired. I called Legal Seafoods and asked for a reservation for two, only to be told that they did not accept reservations. Knowing what it would be like on a Friday evening in Boston, I explained that my guest for dinner was Virginia Henderson, a very famous and very elderly nurse and begged them to make an exception. The young woman on the phone hesitated, then agreed to a reservation at seven. We arrived exactly at seven and, once again, walked through a waiting area abundant with nurses who acknowledged my dinner companion with reverent nods and smiles. The hostess looked up and immediately knew who we were. She greeted us with, "Good evening, Miss Henderson. Let me show you to your table." Virginia Henderson's eyes twinkled.

Comfortably seated, water poured, and drinks ordered, we were approached by a very handsome young waiter who told us about "the specials." The minute that he and Virginia Henderson made eye contact, she dropped me like a hot potato and proceeded to flirt mercilessly with this young man. She sparkled all over as she explained to him (in her wonderful southern accent that she never lost in all those years in New England) that she was deathly allergic to onions and that she was relying on him to assure that none of her food would come into contact with an onion. He resonated to this investment of trust and assured her that he would personally oversee the preparation of her food. This was the beginning of a 2-hour love affair between an extraordinary elderly woman and a delightful young man. My role was simply the foil and the observer. And as I watched this wonderful and touching flirtation, I was projected momentarily into my own nineties and only hoped that I would have the glow, the luster, and radiance that I witnessed in Virginia Henderson that evening.

Eventually, we finished our excellent dinner, attended by our doting and by now, devoted server. Evidently, he had alerted the rest of the staff to Miss Henderson's charm and we were visited by the maitre d'hôtel and others. She knew she had captivated them all and became even more enchanting. I was tickled to see that Miss Henderson saw no need to avoid the endangered pleasure of dessert and we had a high-fat, high-calorie, delicious one. I think perhaps she really did not want our dinner to end. After a delightful conversation in the taxi back to the hotel, Miss Henderson was greeted and whisked away by other adoring fans. As we parted in the lobby, I felt both joyful and content. It was a vintage evening, never to be forgotten.

It would be difficult to think of a single educator in this century who has inspired more nurses and more profoundly influenced our profession. She probably would have said that she had a longer time in which to do it than some of the others. Nevertheless, her definition of nursing, her textbook, her social activism all are components of an inspirational whole for nurses past, present, and future. But to say that she was a role model for the nursing community misses the point. My evening with Virginia Henderson convinced me that her uniqueness was her strength. She didn't just seem to struggle with the banality that is so familiar to the rest of us—juggling child rearing with tenure with publishing. She was singular, peerless, an icon in nursing; not to be copied or modeled or imitated, but rather to be treasured. She was, and is, a jewel or a work of art, timeless and immortal, from whom we will forever derive deep satisfaction, inspiration, and enlightenment. I remember once one of my anthropology professors, in a lecture about the relationship between individual and culture, observed that we all grow old and die, except for some charming women who live forever. I cherish the memory of my evening with Miss Virginia Henderson, who, in my mind, will live forever.

Moments

Daniel James, BS, RN
Hospice Home Care Nurse
Connecticut Hospice Incorporated
Branford, CT

C***ommitting to paper*** the influence that another person has had on your life is not an easy task. And what challenges me further is that this person I'm about to write about was Virginia Henderson. I am not a Yale colleague or life-long friend. I am distinct by the fact that I was Virginia's hospice home care nurse.

I therefore feel her influence on me was rather unique. I do not remember Virginia as "teacher," "speaker," or "fellow-researcher." I remember her as one of my patients. And not unlike some of the very special people I have cared for, she has in her own way had an impact on me both professionally and personally.

In the course of my work, there are so many people who have crossed my life's path. Due to its very nature, hospice care forges relationships that are inherently short and intense. My relationship with Virginia was no exception.

Not uncommon to the human experience, Virginia was frail and forgetful in the last half-year of her life. This is where our relationship began. Amidst the difficulties in communicating, I could easily feel her essence. She always made you feel welcomed. She was easy to be with.

I remember the afternoon when her referral came to home care. My supervisor pulled me aside to ask if I would take the case. The referral had been handed to her from the upper echelons of the Connecticut Hospice. Few referrals come to us this way. I remember not completely connecting the dots when her name was first mentioned. After my supervisor had restored my memory, I began to feel a little nervous. Certainly, any course in nursing history devotes time to Virginia and her work. Where the nineteenth century had Florence Nightingale, we in the twentieth century have Virginia Henderson. What more needs to be said?

Well, word gets around in a small office. Soon, everyone knew who Virginia's primary nurse was going to be. Wouldn't you know, Virginia had a hand in starting the hospice movement here in the United States. Nor would I forget, she was close friends with

Florence Wald, the former dean of the Yale School of Nursing. My colleagues did not leave any "informational stone" unturned.

Frankly, I could have done well with half the information on Virginia that was cheerfully given to me. The anticipated pressure was weighing a bit heavy. I was thankful it wasn't an urgent admission. I would have at least twenty-four hours to prepare myself. It's funny the things that go through your mind. I remember the following day playing out worst-case scenarios in my head. I can direct some Oscar-worthy scenes. One particular daydream filled an auditorium with Virginia's family, friends, and colleagues. The topic of the day. . . my care plan for Virginia. Did I say daydream? I really meant nightmare.

The referral directed me to call Catherine Burdge, Virginia's great niece. Catherine, who is also a registered nurse, was working at Yale. She couldn't meet until she got off work. She was so pleasant to talk to. My fears, although still present, were thankfully not being elevated to new heights. We would meet at The Gables, the assisted living facility in Guilford, Connecticut where Virginia resided.

Catherine had told me that Virginia was partial to male nurses. Being in the minority, I had over the years become hypersensitive to any comments, good or bad, that included "male nurse." A bias, yes, but you could not take this any other way than in the genuine light in which it was shed. Besides, I could use any "ace card" I could get my hands on.

I met Catherine and Virginia at five o'clock in Virginia's second floor apartment. There was no one but the two of them, smiling as I walked in. Virginia's smile was instantly infectious. I joined in smiling as I approached and introduced myself.

The admission was a smooth process and Virginia was particularly alert that evening. I often dread discussing the DNR issue. You never really know where people are in that thought process. Fortunately, Catherine revealed that Virginia had a living will. Signing for the DNR bracelet turned out to be a formality. I applied the bracelet on her right wrist to honor her wish.

Thankfully, Virginia's hospice course was uncomplicated and uneventful. Save for a rare Tylenol to address her arthritic discomfort, she was very comfortable the majority of the time. Catherine always remained focused on maintaining Virginia's independence. I admired that. It was only when safety had become an issue and Virginia was noticeably weaker that she was transferred to the Connecticut Hospice inpatient facility.

It was difficult to carry on a long conversation with Virginia. My visits were short, seeing her about two times per week. There was, however, one particular visit I will always remember—a moment where I felt very connected to her.

During the majority of my visits, I found Virginia sleeping. This particular afternoon, I found her lying on top of her made bed, dressed in her Sunday best, resting peacefully. Calling her name, she awoke easily. She then slowly sat up at the edge of the bed. And with her left hand she gently tapped the edge of her bed motioning me to sit down. There we sat. No words were exchanged, for there really was nothing we needed to discuss. She appeared comfortable. I don't think I even took her blood pressure that visit. We both just sat there looking out the window, enjoying the view of the woods.

In that moment, I felt that I had met Virginia Henderson, the person. And, I found that I liked that person very much. After her death, in a reception held in her honor, I watched a taped interview of her taken ten years prior. I then saw her in the way that most people remember her. I was impressed. She appeared so humble in her achievements and so approachable as a person. How comforting it was to know that one of the great leaders of our profession was such a warm and open person. A new fan was born.

I would imagine that, like myself, the boundaries of "the person" and "the nurse" were often blurred for Virginia. That simple gesture of extending herself to me was truly unforgettable. Certainly, this was clearly a manifestation of her warm personality. But, it also rang true to what I feel is the core of being a nurse.

The power of nonverbal communication is undaunting. As nurses, if we are receptive, we can shower ourselves with "moments" such as these. These "moments" are there to enrich our personal and professional lives. I'm forever grateful for that quiet moment I spent with Virginia.

Responsive Prayer

Almighty God, maker of the heavens and the earth and creator of all living things, we have learned to look to you for comfort in every loss. Hear us now as we lift to you our prayers.

For your servant Virginia who recently departed this life,
We give you thanks, O God.

For her unending devotion to family, friends, and nursing colleagues,
We give you thanks, O God.

For her ability to make each of us feel that we were a uniquelyimportant part of her life,
We give you thanks, O God.

For the loving care she gave to her patients as she comforted them, healed them, maintained their health, and saw themto a peaceful death,
We give you thanks, O God.

For her contributions to nursing nationally and internationally, her research, her textbooks, her definition of nursing, and her belief that the profession be recognized as an art and a science,
We give you thanks, O God.

For her infinite wisdom, quiet strength, constant love, and courageous compassion,
We give you thanks, O God.

For her spiritual beliefs and her respect for those of others,
We give you thanks, O God.

For her ability to bring the world of nursing together through her travels and her love of humanity,
We give you thanks, O God.

For her ability to inspire us, challenge us, nurture us, and encourage us as we sought her guidance both in personal and professional endeavors,
We give you thanks, O God.

For the beautiful care that she received as she neared the end of her life,
We give you thanks, O God.

Grant us grateful hearts and unfailing memories of dear Virginia who has touched our lives forever,
We ask this in your great wisdom, O God.

Written by Catherine M. Burdge, great niece of Virginia A. Henderson, for the Service of Thanksgiving and Remembrance for Virginia A. Henderson held at Battell Chapel, Yale University, New Haven, CT, USA on May 6, 1996.

Appendices

Virginia Avenel Henderson
Biographical Notes

I. Personal

- Born November 30, 1897 in Kansas City, Missouri, the fifth of eight children of Lucy Abbot Henderson and attorney Daniel B. Henderson.
- Her given names, Virginia Avenel, honor her mother's home state and dear friends of her mother who lived in a house called Avenel in Bedford, Virginia.
- Family relocated to Virginia in 1901 where she grew to adulthood.
- Died March 19, 1996 in Branford, Connecticut.

II. Education

- Received early education at home and at school for boys run by her uncle, Charles Abbot, in Virginia.
- Initial professional education took place at Army School of Nursing at Walter Reed Hospital (diploma, 1921); followed by baccalaureate degree (1932) and master of arts degree in nursing education (1934) from Teachers College, Columbia University, New York, New York.

III. Practice and Teaching

- Staff Nurse, Visiting Nurse Associations of New York City and Washington, DC (1921-1923).
- Instructor and Educational Director, Norfolk Protestant Hospital School of Nursing, Norfolk, Virginia (1924-1929).
- Clinical Instructor, Outpatient Department, Strong Memorial Hospital and School of Nursing, University of Rochester, Rochester, New York (1930-1931).
- Instructor and Associate Professor of Nursing Education, Teachers College, Columbia University, New York, New York (1934-1948).

IV. Research and Writing

- Research Associate, Yale University School of Nursing, New Haven, Connecticut. Staff of *Nursing Research: A Survey and Assessment* project directed by Leo W. Simmons (1953-1958); Director, *Nursing Studies Index* project (1959-1971).
- Research Associate Emeritus, Yale University School of Nursing, New Haven, Connecticut (1971-1996).
- Authored more than 40 articles, chapters, editorials, forewords, and book reviews,

in addition to 11 books, including the four-volume *Nursing Studies Index*. Selected writings were translated and published in many languages.

V. Consultation

- Traveled extensively throughout the United States giving lectures, workshops, seminars, and "conversations."
- After her so-called retirement at the age of 75, served as a consultant to nurses, schools of nursing, and nursing organizations on four of the world's seven continents (Australia, Canada, Denmark, England, France, Ireland, Israel, Japan, Norway, Pakistan, Scotland, Spain, Switzerland, Wales).

Virginia Avenel Henderson
Major Awards

1970 Achievement Award in Nursing Practice. As an educator, researcher, and practitioner. Nursing Education Alumnae Association. Teachers College, Columbia University, New York, New York.

1971 Commendation. For dedication to the advancement of the profession and outstanding contributions to nursing education and practice. Connecticut Nurses Association.

1974 Distinguished Service Award. For distinguished and exemplary service, nursing leadership, and social consciousness in furthering the worthy cause of nursing and health care. American Nurses Association.

1976 Presidential Bicentennial Award. Boston College, Chestnut Hill, Massachusetts.

1977 Mary Adelaide Nutting Award. For leadership in nursing education. National League for Nursing.

1980 Virginia A. Henderson Award. For outstanding contributions to nursing research. Connecticut Nurses Association.

1981 Annie W. Goodrich Award. For excellence in teaching. Yale University School of Nursing Student Body. New Haven, Connecticut.

1982 R. Louise McManus Medal. Nursing Education Alumnae Association. Teachers College, Columbia University, New York, New York.

1983 Mary Tolle Wright Founders Award. For excellence in leadership. Sigma Theta Tau.

1985 Christiane Reimann Prize. For outstanding contributions to nursing worldwide. International Council of Nurses.

1985 Promotion of Research in Nursing Practice Award. School of Nursing, State University of New York, Buffalo, New York.

1985 Commendation. For contributions to library and information resources for nursing. The Nursing and Allied Health Source Section of the Medical Library Association, New York, New York.

1985 Meritorious Service Award. National Association of Nurses of Colombia, South America.

1985 Excellence in Education Award. (Now named Virginia Henderson Award.) National Association of Home Care.

1985 Luther P. Christman Award. For continued support of men in nursing. American Assembly for Men in Nursing.

1987 Vice-President for Life. Royal College of Nursing. London, England.

1987 Certificate of Appreciation. Interagency Council on Library Resources for Nursing.

1988 Distinguished Service Medal. Teachers College, Columbia University, New York, New York.

1988 Award. l'Escola d'Infermeria de la Universtat de Barcelona, Spain.

1988 Historical Award. In recognition of impact on the development of the nursing profession and the health care provided citizens of the Commonwealth and the country. Virginia Nurses Association.

1988 Special Citation of Honor. "'The world's most beloved nurse.' Your dedication, vision and leadership have inspired generations of nurses." American Nurses Association.

1989 Presidential Award. In recognition of the contributions, time, and work given to the Honor Society of Nursing. Sigma Theta Tau International.

1990 Certificate of Appreciation. New England Regional Council on Library Resources for Nursing.

1990 Sigma Theta Tau International Library named in honor of Virginia Henderson. Indianapolis, Indiana.

1996 Inducted into American Nurses Association Hall of Fame. For leadership that affected the health and/or social history of the United States through sustained life-long contributions in or to nursing practice, education, administration, research, economics, or literature, and for achievements of enduring value to nursing beyond her lifetime. American Nurses Association. Washington, DC.

1996 Virginia Henderson Clinical Research Award Endowment established by Sigma Theta Tau International.

Virginia Avenel Henderson
Honorary Degrees

1970	Doctor of Laws	*University of Western Ontario* *London, Ontario, Canada*
1972	Doctor of Science	*University of Rochester* *Rochester, New York*
1975	Doctor of Science	*Rush University* *Chicago, Illinois*
1979	Doctor of Humane Letters	*Pace University* *New York, New York*
1980	Doctor of Science	*Catholic University of America* *Washington, DC*
1982	Doctor of Science	*Yale University* *New Haven, Connecticut*
1983	Doctor of Science	*Old Dominion University* *Norfolk, Virginia*
1983	Doctor of Science	*Boston College* *Chestnut Hill, Massachusetts*
1985	Doctor of Letters	*Thomas Jefferson University* *Philadelphia, Pennsylvania*
1985	Doctor of Science	*Emory University* *Atlanta, Georgia*
1986	Doctor of Humane Letters	*Saint Joseph College* *West Hartford, Connecticut*
1988	Doctor of Science	*University of North Carolina* *Greensboro, North Carolina*

Virginia Avenel Henderson
Honorary Associations

1973 Honorary membership. Yale University School of Nursing Alumnae/i Association, New Haven, Connecticut.

1975 Honorary membership. Registered Nurses Association of Ontario, Canada.

1977 Honorary fellowship. American Academy of Nursing.

1977 Honorary membership. Association of Integrated and Degree Courses in Nursing, England.

1977 Honorary membership. Irish Nurses Association, Dublin, Ireland.

1978 Honorary fellowship. Royal College of Nursing of the United Kingdom.

1979 Honorary membership. Iota chapter, Sigma Theta Tau, Vanderbilt University School of Nursing, Nashville, Tennessee.

1983 Honorary life membership. Alberta Association of Registered Nurses, Canada.

1985 Honorary membership. Japanese Nursing Association, Tokyo, Japan.

1987 Honorary membership. Norwegian Nurses Association, Norway.